my life as
a matador

Bradley Conrad

my life as a matador

THE AUTOBIOGRAPHY OF

carlos arruza

WITH BARNABY CONRAD

illustrated

HOUGHTON MIFFLIN COMPANY BOSTON

THE RIVERSIDE PRESS CAMBRIDGE

Books by Barnaby Conrad

THE INNOCENT VILLA, MATADOR

LA FIESTA BRAVA

Library of Congress catalogue card number: 56-7446.

Second Printing December 1956

The selection from *The Collected Papers of Otto Fenichel,* edited by Hannah Fenichel and David Rapaport, is reprinted by permission of the publishers, W. W. Norton and Company, Inc. The quotation from an article on bullfighting by Patricia Hetter is reprinted by permission of the *Journal of Esthetics and Art Criticism.*

The Riverside Press
CAMBRIDGE · MASSACHUSETTS
PRINTED IN THE U.S.A.

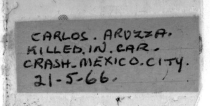

Dedication —

Let it go, then,

for the memory of Manolete

tRanslatoR's
note

I RECENTLY ASKED Don Juan Belmonte, "Does your autobiography please or displease you now?"

His great jaw jutted out and he stammered in that disarming way of his, "I really don't know. It never has occurred to me to r-r-read it."

Belmonte's "autobiography," *Killer of Bulls,* was written by a newspaperman, Chávez Nogales, and translated by a novelist, Leslie Charteris, so although the book captured a fine portrait of the man, it cannot be called a true autobiography.

On the other hand, whereas Belmonte neither wrote nor read his autobiography, Arruza wrote his story out by himself. He took almost a year to do it, writing it in longhand and with a natural style.

At his request I went over the manuscript with him and suggested amplifications or deletions. Then I made this free translation. I have also intruded from time to time with footnotes to help explain some technical matters because, as the brilliant English critic Kenneth Tynan has written, "No public spectacle is more technical, offers less to the untaught observer, than a bullfight."

Therefore, while I have helped with this story, it should be understood that it is not an "as told to" proposition by any matter of means.

B. C.

San Francisco

REX SMITH, probably America's finest
aficionado, has stated in print: "I've
seen them all, from Joselito to Belmonte
to Manolete, and, in my opinion, Carlos
Arruza is the most complete and versa-
tile torero ever to don a suit of lights."

foreword

BY BARNABY CONRAD

I CAME into the grubby hotel room where a handsome, thirty-five-year-old Mexican millionaire, who looks like an American college senior, was preparing himself for possible violent death.

"Hallo, Bernabé," he greeted me as he pulled on the special underwear pants. "Wha's cooking?" He smiled boyishly at his English. "How goes the translation? I want to read about my misdeeds in English." He plugged in his electric shaver and began running it over his face. "Excuse the hotel, but my men feel more at home here than in the fancy ones."

Until his retirement to the Good Life in 1953, Carlos Arruza was the highest paid athlete in the world and possibly the greatest single drawing attraction in the history of bullfighting. Since that time he has devoted himself to the raising of bulls for other men to test themselves against and has resisted all astronomic offers for him to return to the ring. He has performed an occasional exhibition fight for charity but eight months ago he broke his arm badly and had to give up all bullfighting. Recently, however, he was talked into appearing in a benefit performance at a border town, and to the lovers of la fiesta brava in both Latin and North America this Sunday was an event of great importance.

All morning there had been a steady procession of Cadillacs, Lincolns, and Jaguars moving sleekly across the river from El Paso and San Antonio and Dallas and even California, for there was a feeling of urgency and compulsion in the air; an expert in the most dangerous of all the arts, perhaps the finest in his field who ever lived, was once more going to demonstrate skills which he had learned over a tumultuous twenty-two-year career. Many Americans who weren't at all sure they liked bullfighting were going simply because of "this fellow Ahrootzah," because they wanted to see The Best, no matter what his line, and they knew this might be their last opportunity. Only a few knew about his arm, that when it had healed the contracted tendons left it bowed six inches shorter than the other. I watched him working it now as he finished shaving.

"How is it?" I asked.

"Fine," he said, "just fine." He gave a mirthless laugh.

"Maybe I could place my own banderillas today, if we just made one of the sticks six inches shorter. Or better still, let's make one of the horns six inches shorter." Then he held out his arms, comparing their length, as though to see if the tendons might have loosened up magically since he last looked at them five minutes before. He shook his head. "This was a crazy idea, this fight."

He sat on the unmade bed and leafed through a Dick Tracy comic book in Spanish. Someone sent up a watercolor painting of Arruza doing his pass, the arrucina, to be autographed, and he borrowed a pen from me to sign it. Then he went back to Dick Tracy. He sipped his coffee, the only nourishment he'd take before the fight so that he could be operated upon immediately if he was gored. Then he slapped the comic book down, got up and moved around the room nervously, but with the easy animal grace of an ocelot.

Even though he does no dieting he has gained only four pounds since he retired. His build is still the ideal of any taurine tailor, for he is thin, hipless, broad-shouldered, and tall. The perfection of his body is marred by his bad left arm and by the long white scars that pucker his legs and groin. He has been relatively lucky, because he has been fighting professionally since he was thirteen years old, killing an amazing 1260 bulls, and has only been gored seriously seven times. (Belmonte, dean of Spanish matadors, estimates his critical cornadas at over fifty.)

Arruza also has a vicious eight-inch scar that jags around the back of his neck up to his left ear, but this came when a taxi driver went berserk after a minor collision with Arruza's car and suddenly knifed him. ("I tell American tourists that it was a giant Miura bull," says Arruza. "It sounds more romantic.")

Now Vargas, his gray-haired sword boy, helped worry him into the tight trousers of his traje corto costume. He hadn't put on the frilled shirt yet, and the gold medallions from the five chains around his neck shone against the tan of his chest. He buttoned the trousers and then looked down out of the window at the hot streets of the town already bristling and tense with the excitement of the fight. With his right hand gripping his left shoulder Arruza kept working his bad arm, like a boxer stabbing out at a punching bag.

"This was about as crazy an idea as I ever had," he said.

I was there when it all started a week before with the ring of the phone in the den of his luxurious penthouse in Mexico City. The call was an appeal to help a veteran banderillero, Campanero, who was destitute and sick with cancer of the throat.

"Matador, we could raise $20,000 with just one bullfight."

Arruza twisted the telephone cord and protested. "But I'm retired — how about some young active bullfighter?"

"Nobody but you can fill a bullring — at the prices we're going to charge. We've got to help old Campanero."

"But my arm! It's still no good. I can't do it. I'm sorry."

He hung up. Running his fingers through his dark brown hair, he walked unhappily around the den. The walls are covered with photographs and trophies, and there is an original ink drawing by Picasso of Arruza with wings fighting a bull also with wings and an inscription to him which starts out: "A corrida of angels . . ."

Arruza tapped the glass of one photograph. "Campanero," he said. "This was when I was just a novillero. He was my manager then. How that little man loved to talk. Imagine the irony of this: now they have removed his tongue and larynx, and he never learned how to write, so he can't even talk that way." He blew out a sigh. Then he went back to the telephone and dialed.

"All right," he said into the phone. "Let's try it."

He hung up, looked at me, and shrugged. "Well. Let's go out to the ranch and pick out some bulls."

Arruza's wife came to the door of the den with their two-year-old son. She is a chic young Spanish girl named María del Carmen, called Mari, which is pronounced MAH-ree. It was for her that Arruza retired; she had lost three babies and the doctor said she would never be able to hold one while worrying whether or not Carlos was going to be gored that afternoon or not. They have two small boys now.

"We're going shopping," she said. "In *that* car."

Carlos had given her a new Studebaker the day before for her saint's day. "Try to wait a few days before cracking it up, mi vida," he said grinning. They call each other "my life."

"Look who's talking," she said with her good smile. "He

who cracked up the Rolls. Oh, I forgot to tell you the Silvetis
are coming in for Canasta tonight."

"Fine," said Arruza, as he stood up and put on his gabar-
dine coat. He hesitated. Then he said casually, "Oh, Mari —
would you mind having my traje corto pressed."

Mari's smile faded. "That corrida they called about
yesterday!"

"It's not a corrida, just a festival."

"You're going to fight?"

"Yes."

"And your arm?"

"It'll be fine." Carlos held out both arms in front of him,
purposely shortening his right arm so that the two looked
almost the same length. "See what El Brujo has done?"
Arruza has gone to several doctors in Mexico City before he
finally switched to a chiropractor called "the Wizard" who,
Carlos claims, has done wonders for his arm.

"You can't fight with that arm. I thought Tijuana was
the last."

"It's for charity, mi vida. For old Campanero."

"The bulls don't know that."

"They'll be small. Almost calves."

"Hah," said Mari.

At that moment little Carlitos shook his coat like a cape and said: "Ah-hah, toro!"

Carlos laughed, made his fingers like horns, and charged the delighted boy once. Then Carlos kissed Mari, and said, "See you when we get back from the ranch, beautiful!"

She left and a few moments later as we started to go out the front door, El Tarzán came in. A huge man with an incongruous and sublimely angelic face, he was Arruza's favorite picador for years. When a bull injured his spine and he could no longer ply his trade of wearing down bulls with a vara, Carlos made him his secretary.

"Hola, Tarzancito," said Carlos affectionately. "Did you get it done?"

He made
his fingers like
horns.

"Yes, Matador, but he wants to pay with a check."

"Tell him he either pays cash or the bulls don't leave the ranch. And call Chucho and tell him we'll pick him up at the Palace right away." Carlos gestured to me. "You remember Bernabé."

"Certainly, from Spain days," said Tarzán. Then to Carlos, "Matador, you have an appointment with Gaona at eleven tomorrow and a golf lesson at one. The President and his family and the Archbishop would like to visit the ranch sometime next month and your lawyer wants to talk to you about the lawsuit."

Arruza was suing the Hollywood producers of *The Magnificent Matador* for $65,000 for the injury to his arm. A good deal of the action was shot on his ranch and he was injured while caping a heifer into position for a scene; Arruza claims he warned the assistant director that the rocky terrain was dangerous but that the man stubbornly insisted.

"I want an appointment with El Brujo every day this week," Arruza said. "I'm fighting Sunday."

El Tarzán's fat face went solemn and he looked as though he were going to say something else, but he just nodded and said, "Yes, Matador."

As we went down the seven floors in the elevator Carlos was frowning and holding his arm. "I don't like to worry Mari with this fight. But one must think of old Campanero."

We walked out of the building, which Arruza purchased in 1948 for $200,000, into the glare of Balderas Street and got into the big gray Rolls-Royce at the curb. (Carlos employs a chauffeur, but seldom lets him drive.) We rolled smoothly into the heavy traffic of Avenida Juárez and shortly we stopped in front of a hole-in-the-wall restaurant known as Paco Llopis' Palace Café.

"My office," said Carlos with a grin. A pretty girl asked for an autograph while her escort looked bored, and then we went in to the dim drab bar through the frijoles-scented kitchen, and into a small private room whose walls were lined with photographs of Arruza in action, as well as other retired or dead greats such as Silverio, Solórzano, Manolete, Balderas, and Gaona. There were four men already playing dominoes as they sipped their coffee, plus several kibitzers.

"Hola, Matador," said the Spanish torero, Antonio Durán, reverently. "Buenos días," said the others.

"Hey, Carlos," said the gypsy Cagancho, one of the great matadors of all time, "tell these bums that my ancestors left me more money than they ever dreamed of — only trouble is it's all stashed away over there in the Pharaohs' tombs and I can't lay my hands on it!"

They all laughed because Cagancho is popular and any jokes about gypsies will usually amuse toreros.

We had coffee and Arruza made derogatory comments on the play of the men, which were parried good-humoredly. In a few moments Chucho Solórzano came in. One of Arruza's best friends, tall, bald, and distinguished-looking, Solórzano could be passed off quicker as a Manhattan stock broker than he could as one of Mexico's greatest ex-matadors. Retired for ten years and a wealthy ranch owner, Chucho now is a three-goal polo player with the top team of the Gracida brothers. He had just returned from matches in Hawaii.

"Why do you insist upon dressing like my grandfather?" said Arruza, fingering the lapel of Solórzano's Brooks Brothers suit.

Chucho snorted at this running gag of Carlos'. "It's better than your zoot suits."

As we left, Arruza said to the others: "See you later, gentlemen." Arruza manages to make the Palace at least twice a day and feels his day is not complete unless he plays four games of dominoes with the pandilla — the gang. Mari, like any other club widow, fails to see the allure of the place. The truth is that Carlos prefers a proletarian atmosphere such as the Palace to the swank milieu to which his wealth now gives him access, and he always seeks out friends and surroundings that hark back to his modest beginnings.

We drove out of town toward Toluca. Arruza's car is probably the best known in Mexico and several people waved and two policemen saluted as we headed out on the Pan American Highway. Carlos told Chucho about the bullfight for Campanero.

"And your arm?" Chucho asked.

"Fine," said Arruza. "Just fine."

Chucho snorted.

For the next hour the talk was mostly of sports and bull-fighting. Subjects covered were Toluca's "futbol" (soccer) team, Ava Gardner, "beisbol," Ben Hogan, girl bullfighters (Arruza's pet hate), Mexico's champion boxer Ratón Macías, this new star novillero Chamaco, and the disagreement between the union of the Spanish and Mexican matadors. (All phases of bullfighting are completely unionized, from picadors to sweepers of the arena sand.) Chucho kept urging Carlos to take up polo seriously. Carlos has only played a few times but Chucho and the Gracida brothers say he could be playing championship polo in six months. "The greatest natural athlete I have ever seen," says Chucho.

In 1945 in Spain I saw Arruza pick up a tennis racket for the first time in his life, play in a foursome with superb form, and astonish the tennis pro of the club. In spite of his bad arm he is doing the same thing to the golf pro in Mexico City, who claims he has never seen such a natural swing. Last year he won the water skiing trophy in Acapulco three weeks after his first time on the boards.

Sporting terms sprinkle most of Arruza's conversations. When Chucho said "My wife tells me Mari's expecting another baby," Carlos answered, "Yes, he's rounding second base already."

At one point I asked, "How about Carlitos — is he going to be a matador too?"

Carlos shot me a sidelong "you-kidding?" glance. "My son will be an industrious, conservative, scientific agriculturist" — he winked — "like his old man."

As we arrived in Toluca, a neat white town of 60,000, the conversation had switched to the late great Manolete. When Arruza went into the bank I asked Chucho, "How would you compare Arruza with Manolete?"

He replied thoughtfully. "The five greatest toreros of the twentieth century were Gaona, Joselito, Belmonte, Manolete, and Arruza. The best? Matter of taste. Like choosing between Corbett, Dempsey, Tunney, Marciano, and Louis. Me, I happen to think Arruza was."

"And Arruza retired and with a bad arm?"

Chucho shrugged. "We'll see Sunday."

Twenty minutes out of Toluca we came to the flat fertile fields that mark the beginning of Pastejé, the four-thousand-acre ranch which Arruza bought in 1953 for one million dollars cash, U.S. currency. Pastejé, which means "grazing land" in Indian, has been famous for breeding fighting bulls for the arena for twenty-five years. We saw a few cows and bulls out in the fields on either side of the highway, but Arruza said, with a touch of scorn in his voice, "Mansos."

Manso means "tame" and is a word used to distinguish domestic cattle from the true Toro Bravo, which is a separate breed raised for only one purpose: to try to kill men. Arruza has 700 head of cattle at Pastejé, most of which are fighting stock. On the other hand, the quarter-of-a-million dollar ranch that he owns in Spain is predominantly made up of domestic cattle.

As we drove off the highway and up a dirt road toward the

red and white hacienda buildings, we saw the line of ninety-three Holstein cows being herded in.

"Imported from the Carnation people up in the States," said Carlos proudly. "Several of my cows give forty liters a day!" Then he added in English, "I don't believe it, I don't believe it!" He likes to lace his conversations with English phrases, learned at the American grammar school he attended in Mexico City, and this is his favorite at the moment, although it comes out "Ah done blibit."

We drove past Arruza's private jai alai court, the chapel, the sheds with the big farming machinery, into the courtyard, and parked in front of the main building, where we were met by some tame deer, Carlos' German shepherd dog Sudi, and two of the staff. Arruza employs fifteen hands permanently, but at harvest time he takes on 200 more — at twenty American cents a day per person.

The main building is a quadrangle with thirteen bedrooms and bathrooms, plus dining and living rooms, all giving out on to a lawned patio with a blue-tiled fountain in the center. Servants showed us to our rooms down the arcade, where at regular intervals there are framed the big gaudy posters from memorable Arruza fights. The walls of the room where I changed my clothes were covered with dozens of violent photographs of Arruza being tossed by different bulls throughout his career. Carlos had lettered a little sign in Spanish:

> *These unpleasant moments helped to pay*
> *For a certain ranch named Pastejé.*

Arruza came out of his room shortly, dressed in the traditional charro outfit of the Mexican cowboy. When Sudi bounded around him barking playfully, Carlos took off his big sombrero and holding it in his left hand he said, "Whuh-

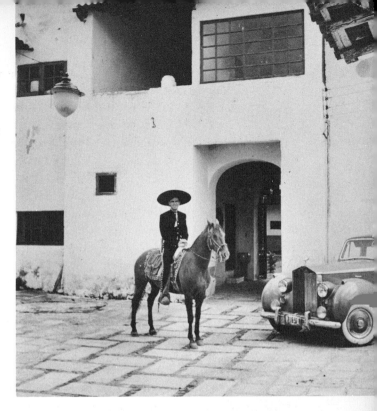

Entrance to the main building of Pastejé.

hey, toro!" The "bull" charged and Carlos tried to swing his arm, but it jerked stiffly halfway through the pass. He put his hat back on his head and patted the dog.

The horses were saddled and waiting. Chucho and Carlos and I trotted off, with photographer Juan Guzmán and the overseer bouncing behind us in a jeep. We rode down past the small private bullring that is set in among the big trees one hundred yards from the main house. It is here where Carlos likes to get down in the arena and practice his cape-work with the young animals. The people who think that bullfighters are exhibitionistic sadists should see a torero without an audience, when he does not injure the animals in any way, reveling as he executes the beautiful plastic movements that make up his art. These encounters are not without danger, for a toro bravo at any age is dangerous; a month-old calf will try to attack a man with no provocation whatsoever. One of the worst horn wounds the great Juan Belmonte ever received was while practicing with two-year-old heifers.

"It's a good way for us ex-matadors to let off steam," said Chucho as we rode out past the fields of high green corn. "It's all very well this polo and jai alai and water skiing and driving fast cars, but once a person has known the thrill of making a bull pass by his legs there is no other excitement in the world to compare with it."

We rode out half a mile to the big north field and looked over seventy-five young bulls, some of which were old enough to be shipped to any of the twenty or so principal arenas in Mexico. Carlos sells approximately sixty-five bulls a year to impresarios at an average price of $700 apiece. However, the bull-raising end of the ranch, although Carlos' main interest, constitutes only one-tenth the yearly income produced by the rest of the farm activities.

El toro bravo has a strong herd instinct and as long as he is not separated he is not likely to attack you out in the open. Nevertheless, we stayed a healthy distance from them and moved on quickly whenever we saw one focusing his attention too fixedly on our horses or on the jeep. In a short-distance chase a fighting bull can overtake any horse, and there are many accounts of their overturning and demolishing cars.

The ancestors of the animals we were looking at were *Bos taurus ibericus,* a peculiarly bellicose breed of bovine originally found only on the Iberian Peninsula, where they ran wild like savage beasts. The ancient Romans were among the first to appreciate their deadliness and imported them for their Colosseum games. For centuries man has carefully bred them in Spain and Latin America for the single purpose of combat in the arena. They are not trained in any way, and except for branding, their only pre-arena encounter with man is when they are two years old. Then they are tested by letting them attack a picador on a padded horse, who pricks them with a lance, and their bravery is carefully rated according to how many times they are willing to charge in spite of the sting of the pic. Cowardly bulls are marked for the slaughterhouse and the brave ones are cat-alogued and allowed to develop unmolested until they are around four years old. Testing of the cows for breeders is of the greatest importance, since experts claim that "fight-ing bulls inherit their size from papa but the courage of their hearts from mama."

The bulls are descended principally from imported Span-ish seed bulls of the famous Murube strain, and Pastejé is among the top four of the thirty-odd bull ranches in Mexico. However, Carlos is worried about the future of the gana-dería, since the strain is becoming inbred and no more bulls may be imported from Spain because of the hoof and mouth disease epidemic.

We rode around the herd for half an hour while Arruza picked out the six best-looking animals, writing down their brand numbers on a piece of paper. Besides the number, which is branded large on their sides, the bulls have on their hips the Pastejé brand, a Y design in a circle. ("Just like Mercedes-Benz radiator caps," says Arruza happily.)

Arruza handed the paper to his foreman, who checked the numbers and nodded. These animals would be shipped by truck and in special iron-reinforced crates for Sunday's fight.

Photographer Guzmán in the jeep said, "Why don't you cape one of these animals now so that we can get some photos?"

"If you buy it afterwards," said Carlos. Bullfights are conceived in the theory that this is a bull's first and only real encounter with a dismounted man; bulls that have been caped before learn and remember and cannot be sent into a regulation ring. Therefore, except for their meat, they are worthless.

He turned to me with his boyish grin, "How about it, Bernabé? You buy it and we'll both fight it."

"If you promise to give me a tubercular one," I said. "I haven't fought anything for four years."

Carlos picked out one of the smallest animals in the herd.

"Bring him in," Carlos ordered. "We'll cape him in the little ring later. And you may kill him, Bernabé."

We rode back to the ranch, peons took our horses, and we went into the living room for sherry. While we were waiting for luncheon to be announced, Arruza paced restlessly, then turned on the TV set and watched the antics of Gordo and Flaco (Laurel and Hardy are called "Fat and Thin" south of the border). The living room and adjoining bar are filled with mounted bullheads, gold and silver trophies won by

Arruza watches as Conrad practices a molinete pass in the private arena.

Arruza, and posters and photographs of Arruza in action. There are also several photos of Arruza's brother, Manolo.

Most matadors come from bullfighting forebears and from hungry-poor country folk. Arruza's sophisticated mother and his father, both of whom were successful in the clothing business, were from citified Spanish families who never had anything to do with the bulls. Yet Manolo and Carlos, to the horror of their parents, went to bullfighting school and were fighting as professional becerristas — calf fighters — by the time they were thirteen and fourteen.

Arruza does not tell us in his autobiography the basic motivations for his sudden great determination and fascination with bullfighting, and perhaps he himself does not know them. Much mystic claptrap has been ascribed to the reasons men fight bulls, from religion to homosexuality to thwarted matricide, and perhaps in rare instances it has some validity. But in Arruza's case, and I believe in the cases of the majority of men who get a supreme thrill from "making a bull pass by their legs," the basic underlying reasons are

Arruza demonstrates his fantastic pass "El Péndulo" with the young bull.

contained in this excerpt from the excellent paper entitled "The Counter-Phobic Attitude" by the late psychiatrist Otto Fenichel: *

When the organism discovers that it is now able to overcome without fear a situation which would formerly have overwhelmed it with anxiety, it experiences a certain kind of pleasure. This pleasure has the character of "I need not feel anxiety any more."

. . . The counter-phobic attitude may really be regarded as a never-ending attempt at the belated conquest of an unmastered infantile anxiety.

. . . The most outstanding example is probably the entire field of sport, which may in general be designated as a counter-phobic phenomenon. No doubt there are erotic and aggressive gratifications in sports just as they are present in all the other functional pleasures of adults. Certainly not everyone who engages in sport is suffering from an unconscious insoluble fear of castration, nor does it follow that the particular sport for which he shows a later preference must once have been feared. But it will generally hold true that the essential joy in sport is that one actively brings about in play certain tensions which were formerly feared, so that one may enjoy the fact that now one can overcome them without fearing them.

I am convinced that the reasons for one's taking up bull-fighting are usually neither more nor less neurotic or mystical than those which propel a man to take up high-diving, mountaineering, giant slalom, or sports car racing.

Whatever the reasons, Carlos, and to a lesser degree, Manolo, were caught up in this obsession to fight bulls at an

---

* From *The Collected Papers of Otto Fenichel*, Hannah Fenichel and David Rapaport, eds. (New York: W. W. Norton Co., 1954).

early age. Child prodigies, they fought together for years, and Manolo's death in 1941 is the big tragedy of Carlos' life. He died of a pistol wound, but whether it happened when he was examining the pistol or whether it was suicide or whether someone else was responsible only the family know, and they do not discuss it.

The only other bullfighter whose photograph appears on the ranch is the late Spaniard Manolete, and there are several large ones of him in the little barroom. Arruza was from the beginning of his career a good and natural torero, but it was not until he saw the Spanish master fight in Lisbon in 1944 that he really found himself.

"I never knew anyone could work with a bull in terrains like that," Carlos says. "I never believed it possible that a man could cross the angle of charge that far, then stand still and pass the horns so close."

He set about immediately to adapt this new conception of

The barroom with a poster of Manolete on the wall.

Manolete's to his own fluid and flashy style. He took Spain
by storm that summer. "El Ciclón" they dubbed him, because of his whirlwind rise to fame, and the newspapers
wrote that this was the best Mexican bullfighter to come to
the mother country since Gaona at the beginning of the
century. Great crowds would follow him through the streets,
and fans in the balconies of theaters tied neckties together
so they could lower cards for Arruza, on the main floor, to
autograph. Songs were written about him, five books pub-
lished on him, statues erected, and a liqueur named "Anís
Arruza" became popular instantly

The first time I ever saw Arruza I attended the fight with
Don Juan Belmonte. We went very skeptically, because the
propaganda which had proceeded El Ciclón was like nothing
ever known on the Iberian Peninsula. A sensational buildup,
it had the smell of paid publicity about it. That afternoon
Arruza looked green but good. He was willing, courageous,

Arruza taking Spain by storm in 1944 and 1945.

and inventive, and he was conceded an ear off his last bull. As we left the ring I asked Don Juan what he thought of the new *fenómeno*. Belmonte's barracuda jaw came out as he said in that wonderfully disarming stutter of his: "Pues, el chico no me ha convencido — the lad d-d-didn't convince me."[*]

The next time Arruza had improved vastly, and he cut an ear off one bull and both ears off the second. I asked Belmonte again. "He hasn't c-c-convinced me" was the answer.

The next appearance was in Cádiz when Arruza, entirely alone on the program, killed four bulls. On the first he was awarded both ears, on the second, a lap around the ring, on the third both ears and tail, and on the last, both ears, tail, and a hoof. As we left the ring in the midst of a delirious mob, I asked Belmonte again.

[*] Bullfighters are notoriously chary with compliments for others in their profession. Ask a torero who's the greatest and he will always start out his answer, "Well, *second* there's —" Recently a friend asked the great Spaniard Dominguín to name the ten best matadors of all time. He did after putting his name first. "You didn't include Arruza," my friend protested. "That acrobat!" Dominguín sneered. My friend then went to Dominguín's arch-rival Arruza and asked him to name his ten. Arruza did and added that he'd be hypocritical if he didn't put himself in there someplace too. "You didn't mention Dominguín," my friend pointed out. "Look," said Arruza, "you said ten — not fifty!"

Arruza "convincing" the audience.

His jaw jutted out. He scratched it. He lit a cigar. He shook his head twice. Finally he said, "You know, this l-l-l-lad's beginning to convince me!"

Manolete and Arruza were paired off, and this became the greatest attraction since the Golden Age of Bullfighting back in 1914, when the Joselito-Belmonte rivalry started. All Spain was divided as to who was the greater: Manolete, "The knight of the sorrowful countenance" with his tragic, classic style, or this new young Mexican with his great bravery, freshness, and seemingly endless repertoire. They had a national voting, conducted by a newspaper, to ascertain which was the more popular, and though it was close Arruza won.

I tried to pin down Belmonte as to which he thought was the better but all he would say was, "El que más cobre!" — the one who gets paid the most money.

At the end of the season, Arruza was gored, but he returned the next year for probably the most triumphant season ever recorded. Juan Belmonte had fought 109 corridas in Spain in a single six-month period and this record had remained unbeaten since 1919. In 1945 Arruza signed for 154 corridas, but he stopped at 108 out of deference to Belmonte,

The most triumphant season ever recorded.

and the Spaniards loved him for it. For a good performance the presidente of the plaza de toros will award the matador one ear of the dead bull, and both ears in the case of a very good performance. For an outstanding display, the tail is granted. Hoofs had never before been awarded. But out of those 108 fabulous performances (plus four in Mexico), most of which I was lucky enough to witness, he was awarded 219 ears, 74 tails, and 20 hoofs! Such were his triumphs that one Monday the headlines on the Sevilla newspaper read: "Yesterday Arruza did *not* cut ears!"

Belmonte, in his autobiography, explains his own appeal to the public: "Those waging a losing struggle for existence remembered that I had been even more handicapped and had overcome my handicaps. Those aware of being ugly and misshapen consoled themselves with my ugliness and misshapenness. They looked at me and saw me so feeble, so insignificant, so opposite from what one would expect a conquering hero to be, that their own weaknesses seemed much less of an obstacle to overcome." Arruza was the antithesis; he filled to perfection the part of the true, modest, handsome, resourceful hero of boyhood fantasies.

Nineteen-forty-five was the best year of Carlos' life, since it established him as one of the greatest matadors of all time; from then on, except for the competition of Manolete, he was competing mainly against his own previous performances. In 1946 he was charging 10,000 American dollars per corrida, with income taxes taking only about 1½ per cent. His first quarter of a million dollars he turned over to his mother in jewels and real estate, before building up his own fortune. Life looked very good.

Then in 1947 Manolete was killed by a Miura bull. People had always rather expected that Arruza would get killed, taking the chances he did day after day, but the great, sure, calm, stoic Manolete — he wore a cloak of invincibility.

He filled to perfection the part of the ... hero of boyhood fantasies.

Though rivals in the arena, like Joselito and Belmonte they were great friends out of it, and Manolo's death was a terrible blow to Carlos. A few months later he "cut off the pigtail" and quit the ring.

He starred in a Mexican motion picture, but then what was he to do? Only twenty-eight, he had a long time ahead of him in which to do nothing. So for two years he took the obvious route and dedicated himself to the ferocious pursuit of pleasure, featuring those standard ingredients wine, women, and song, and heavily involving certain prominent actresses often associated with top matadors. He flung money away from him on this continual party as though the bills were contaminated. He tried channeling his restless drive to flying airplanes, but he scared himself once too often and gave it up. (Will Rogers said, "We're all ignorant — but not about the same things." This might be paraphrased: "We're all cowards — but about different things.")

Carlos finally discovered there was no substitute, and since he had managed to spend close to a million dollars on this joyride, he used money as an excuse to return to what he loved to do. He returned to the ring greater than ever and charging higher prices per performance than anyone in the history of bullfighting: Manolete had once received an astounding 120,000 pesos for a single performance, but Arruza topped that by 30,000 pesos, an amount which would equal the buying power of about 50,000 dollars in the United States. He married Mari Vázquez, the unsophisticated daughter of a wealthy landowner in Sevilla in 1950, and they had one child, who died. She was unable to have another until his final retirement in 1953.

As we went into luncheon that day at the ranch Chucho said to me, "Marrying Mari was the best thing Carlos ever did. I have known him for a long time and only now do I feel that he is truly happy. This charity fight thing — I wonder if he doesn't wish he had a heart hard enough to have turned it down."

A week later I found myself wondering the same question as I stood in the hotel room in this border town and watched Arruza dressing and trying to work more life into his left arm.

Now it was only half an hour before the Bad Time, the trumpet time, the bull time. The banderillero, Ricardo Aguilar, was already in his costume, and he leaned against the wall of the room smoking nervously, watching his matador dress as he has so many times before. He has worked for him since Arruza was a child performer; the members of his cuadrilla remain Arruza's closest friends, these men who knew him and sweated blood with him for so many years before he became rich and famous.

Earlier in the day, while returning from Mass, playing dominoes, and then going to the drawing of the bulls, there had been a great deal of forced banter and joking. Now there was a strange calm-tenseness in the room. No one exactly whispered, but then neither did they talk very loud.

Arruza took the red sash, and while his sword handler, Vargas, pulled on one end of it, he held the other to his waist and spun twice to wrap it tightly around him. Vargas, with Arruza all through his greatest seasons and now installed as foreman of the ranch, looked excited and worried and happy, somehow all at the same time.

The door was open to the hallway and suddenly a little Victor Moore sort of man appeared there, his throat muffled in a scarf.

"Hola, Campanero!" said Arruza, going to him and clapping an arm around his shoulders. "Couldn't start without you."

He was a pathetic yet appealing figure with no teeth, a ready smile, and haunted eyes. Arruza introduced us, and Campanero silently and exaggeratedly mouthed the words *mucho gusto*. Then he tapped Arruza's arm and held out his own arms, wrinkling his forehead quizzically. Arruza held out his arms in front of him, cheating with his right arm again. "See?" he said loudly. "Perfect!"

Campanero nodded with pleasure and mutely echoed the word, "Perfect."

Vargas said: "Campa, we have a full house today." He made the money sign with his fingers and said in Andaluz dialect, "Mucho parné!"

Campanero smiled and nodded. He looked wistfully

around the room. Then he pantomimed "See you in the ring. God bless you."

"See you later, compadre," said Arruza. When the little man had left Arruza said unhappily, "I don't know why we always shout. He can hear perfectly well. He just can't talk."

"Poor little fellow," said Aguilar. "He hasn't a prayer."

"Maybe they can stop it," Arruza said. "With these new expensive drugs."

Vargas tapped his wrist watch significantly. "Time."

"I-don't-believe-it, I-don't-believe-it," Arruza said incongruously in English.

The sword boy helped him into the tight jacket. Then Arruza crossed the room to the bureau and lit the three votive candles on it. Behind was an icon of the Virgin of the Macarena, Arruza's favorite saint, which is partially scorched; Mari says it once fell into the candles at precisely the same moment at which Carlos received a terrible goring in the arena.

Now Carlos crossed himself devoutly, making a cross of his thumb and first finger and kissing it. "Virgen mia," he whispered, "please — make my arm move right."

Then he turned and put on his hat and said lightly, "We're going to have to go sometime today, so I guess it might as well be now."

As Arruza led his entourage out through the hotel lobby to the car I heard an American girl whisper, "There goes the most beautiful fanny in the Western Hemisphere!"

Arruza slid into the back seat of the rented car and waved once to the crowd as he drove off. His two strongest superstitions are that he must never go to the plaza in one of his own cars and that he must always sit on the left side; ignoring these fears once cost him a critical cornada in the groin, he claims.

As the car pushed its way through the mob in the streets toward the ring, Arruza said, "John Wayne and I are going to build a new ring in Tijuana next year."

Later he pointed over to the slaughterhouse. "People say the bull doesn't have a chance in the plaza. There's where he doesn't have a chance." And: "They want me to go over to Spain this spring to dedicate the new monument to Manolete."

Then there was no talking. When the car arrived behind the bullring, the toreros got out silently and headed for the cuadrilla gate where they would just have time to go first to the chapel and then have one quick cigarette before the trumpet.

The stands were jammed, and the expectant crowd, the majority Americans, were anxious for the proceedings to start. When the band finished the final bleat of "La Virgen de la Macarena" and struck up the traditional parade paso-doble "Cielo Andaluz," a great cheer went up, and the toreros strode out into the sun across the yellow sand like a pride of lions on the veld.

The other two "swords," Silverio and Ortiz, also famous ex-matadors, fought first because of seniority. The crowd was enthusiastic, liked their performances, and applauded hard and frequently.

But they were impatient, for it was El Número Uno whom they had come to see. They cheered when they saw the ring cleared, saw Arruza get his cape right in his hands, and watched as the Gate of Frights creaked open.

The black bull came slamming out of the toril gate, skidding around as it looked for something to drive its needle-sharp horns into. Arruza motioned to Aguilar, who slid through the burladero opening in the fence and went out to give the bull some passes so that his matador could see how it charged and which horn it preferred to hook with.

Arruza sucked in his breath. He watched the animal make its choppy dangerous attacks as Aguilar flared out his cape twice in front of it and then ran for the fence and vaulted over.

"It doesn't see well with one eye," said Arruza grimly to Vargas. "And of course it would be the right eye, just fine for a left hand."

He went through the fence opening and strode out toward the bull, his big magenta cape out in front of him, chanting, "Whuh-hey, toro!"

The crowd wanted to cheer wildly on the first cape passes that Arruza gave, but somehow a scattering of polite applause was all they could muster; the master's verónicas seemed hurried and awkward, especially when the bull charged on the side of his bad arm. As the trumpet blew for the picadors to come in the ring, Arruza came over to the fence, shaking his head at himself.

After the animal charged the picador on his padded nag, Arruza lured the bull away, and as he did he flipped the cape elegantly over his head. Holding it there behind his body he did six gaoneras, working closer to the horn on each one, and when he turned his back and strode away from the bull the crowd broke forth with solid applause. But still there was a let-down feeling. He had been very good, yes, and certainly better than the other two matadors; but the fabulous Arruza should be better than just very good.

The trumpet blew for the banderillas, and when the crowd saw that he wasn't going to place his own banderillas some of them booed, for Arruza is considered the finest banderillero in the world. They didn't stop to think they shouldn't be booing a man who, still incapacitated by his own misfortune, was risking his life, free of charge, for another. They didn't think about his arm, and he didn't point to it, or shrug apologetically, or even seem to hear them.

Arruza and Vargas intent on the problem of the animal in the arena.

When the trumpet blew for the final act, Arruza took the muleta cape and the sword from Vargas, dedicated the bull to Campanero, and then went out into the center of the ring, empty now except for the bull. The short muleta is made for one-handed passes, and Arruza took it in his good right hand, spreading the red cloth with the sword.

"Whuh-hey, toro!" he called at the animal which was fifty feet away. The bull looked at him alertly. When the man gave a tantalizing shake to the muleta it started to walk toward him, and then it broke into a trot, and then into a full, hard, deadly charge straight at him.

Arruza stood like a post, profiled to the charging bull, the muleta held out at arm's length in front of him. Closer and closer the animal came and Arruza, frozen there, his feet together and flat on the sand, watched it come. Then, when the animal was only six feet away, Arruza suddenly swung the muleta back, snapping it, so that it flashed out on the other side of his body. The bull lunged two feet off its

course to the right to attack this new motion, and Arruza, still having moved nothing but his arm, watched calmly as the bull's left horn grazed the back of his legs, actually hitting the cloth of his pants.

A great roar went up from the crowd, for they had witnessed Arruza's own new "pendulum" pass superbly executed. Then began the *olé*'s shouted in unison, for Arruza

followed that péndulo with twenty-two other passes, and twenty-two times it looked as though he would be hit. He was fighting now not for Campanero but for his own love of the art of tauromachy. He had the animal so controlled by the cloth that he could guide it back and forth in any manner he chose, and at one point, to show his domination of the animal, he casually leaned forward, resting his elbow on the bull's forehead and showed the audience another Arruza invention: El Teléfono.

Then he lined up the animal, sighted down the sword's curved blade, and flinging himself between the horns he sank the weapon up to the hilt between the withers. It coughed twice, died on its feet, and then crashed over.

Arruza turned to the roar of the crowd, a lock of hair over his forehead, a pleased little-boy grin on his face.

With the ears of the dead bull in his hands and with Aguilar throwing back the hats and high-heeled shoes and even a pair of lace panties that were thrown down to him by the delirious crowd, Arruza took his triumphant laps around the arena, looking young and happy. It was just like old times. Except that there would be no hard traveling that night to get on to the next corrida in the next town. He could sleep late in the morning and eat a big breakfast.

There would be dozens of autographs to sign and hands to shake, and then he would plane back to Mexico City to his family and to the relatively staid role of a successful rancher. But right now he was once again the top sword in the world, and it was good, it was fine to have a crowd yelling for you. Arruza, basking in the center of the arena, gestured an embrace to every one of them, for after all, they were the ones who had brought him the Good Life — and he was grateful.

What follows now is Arruza's simple and unpretentious telling of what the road to the Good Life was like.

my life as a matador

1

THIS, NOW, will be an account of my life up to the present. I hope that the inside story of the color and the glory and the hell that necessarily are a part of the making of a matador will prove instructive to the reader who is interested in la fiesta brava, since all of these are an integral part of this ancient spectacle. However, to me, in reviewing my life, the most remarkable fact about the story is that it reveals how a fierce, blind drive can pick a man up, carry him toward a single goal, and govern his entire existence.

Where this drive came from I do not know. The motivation was not poverty, as with so many dedicated matadors who claim that "hunger gores more severely than the bulls," for I was born to a normal middle-class couple who, while never rich, were never very poor either. They were Spanish, but after they were married, they came to Mexico City, where I was born thirty-five years ago.

Until I was thirteen I was a happy-go-lucky, wild sort of boy who rather distressed his parents with his purposelessness. My mother, a determined capable modern businesswoman, felt it was time I thought about something a little more serious than just going to the movies or making the soccer team of the American school I attended. However, I'm sure she never intended for me to become as completely dedicated to anything as I suddenly did overnight, to the profession she most loathed in this world.

It happened when my father decided to take me and my older brother Manolo to see our first bullfight. I might say here that any wild tendencies and temperament that I may have are legitimately come by. My father was a real phenomenon. Let me put it this way: had he been born four hundred years ago he would have been an alchemist. To the world he was a good custom tailor in Mexico City — certainly a conservative enough trade — but in his own mind he was an entrepreneur of the top echelon and any day he was going to strike it rich. His main dreams of glory seemed to center around the gaming tables of Monte Carlo. He used to sit there crosslegged in the shop stitching away on a suit, frowning and muttering to himself, and then all of a sudden he would shout: "I've got it!"

He would jump up, scribble down some numbers, multiply by a few more, divide the total, and then leave for Europe the next day with all of his and my mother's savings. A month or so later he would drag himself back, battered but not defeated.

"I know exactly what I did wrong," he'd say.

"You threw all our money away," my mother would say. "That's what you did wrong."

"I've got a new approach I'm going to develop."

Then he would work along for a while in his shop, which actually was quite a sizable business, and go through the motions of being a good father, husband, and head of the household until the bug would bite him again. Three times he went to Monte Carlo with the same results, until finally he gave up trying to understand the whims of the little white ball. Then he started on oil wells. This wasn't exactly his forte either, as he repeatedly found out.

About this time he became a rabid aficionado. I believe that all the color and pageantry in the plaza de toros gave him a release from his own frustrations and ambitions. We would see him come back from a particularly good corrida flushed and excited and hear him describe to my mother the brave feats the toreros had performed, and we begged to be taken to the next one. Finally one wonderful morning he came in brandishing some tickets, saying, "Come on boys — a los toros, a los toros!"

I'll never forget a single detail of it. It was Armillita and Domingo Ortega in a "hand-to-hand" showdown contest. There couldn't have been a better choice for a wide-eyed future torero to see his first time out, for Ortega was Spain's greatest master at the time and Armillita was Mexico's. (Both are still fighting as I write this, the oldest matadors still active. Ortega is white-haired and fifty-two but still one of the greats. A former waiter, he has married two marquesas, has a large estate, and fights now simply because he cannot do otherwise. Armillita went to the top when he was sixteen, stayed there for twenty-five years and never was gored until the year before he retired. Last year his wife ran off with

mingo Ortega   Fermín Espinosa (Armillita)

his money and he returned to the ring briefly and unhappily.)

The natural excitement of going to a spectacle like a
bullfight for the first time became more intense when we
climbed the big stairs and through the arcades and came out
into the stands of the arena. I was struck by the buzzing and
the flashes of light and shade which made up the audience.
The brave strains of music. The vendors' shouts. The smell
of expensive cigar smoke and perfume. The fine ladies
dressed in their best finery. The tourists looking pale and
apprehensive. My father waving to his friends excitedly.

The clock struck four, that clock which for those on the
outside moves so slowly and for those on the inside spins
along at a dizzy speed. For the first time I heard "La
Virgen de la Macarena" and then "Cielo Andaluz" and the
ominous brassy trumpets and those rumbling kettledrums
which my ears were going to hear so many times. And
through the door strode the men, the demigods, dressed in
silk and gold. The commotion swelled, and before my eyes
there paraded men and charging wild beasts and my ears
rang with the screams and the cheers.

Dazedly I clung to my father's hand as we went down the
jammed staircase afterwards. Everything that had happened was engraved on my mind — that wealth of color,
splendor, and excitement had caught me up in a whirlpool
— a vortex from which I never again was to be free. The
pageantry had had its effect on me, and how could it help
but impress a thirteen-year-old boy? But what really struck
me was the tremendous skill of those men. I have always
loved animals, but I saw no cruelty there in the arena, only
the grace and ease of the man's maneuvers and the great
power he had over those nightmarish creatures that blasted
out of the dark tunnel.

I grew up that afternoon — I won't say matured, for ma-

turity is frequently a long time in coming to a torero — but I know I ceased to be a child that day. Why this sudden drive and determination? I don't know. But whatever the reasons, Manolo shared it with me. Happily enough, exactly the same thing had happened to him — that was the best part of all!

Manolo, may he rest in peace, was one year older than I and a model of the perfect student. Whereas I couldn't be bothered with studying, Manolo always received honor grades. But after this glorious revelation in the plaza de toros, Manolo suddenly lost interest in algebra and Latin.

We sat up all night talking about what we'd seen, and even tried to imitate the capework with a sheet. "Let's just junk school altogether and become toreros," Manolo said.

"But they'll never let us."

"They will if we get kicked out of school."

"There are other schools."

"We'll get ourselves kicked out of them all!"

We shook hands on it and started putting our plan into action the following day. Three months later we were expelled from the Cervantes School as "unmanageable in spite of frequent warnings."

There was a fuss at home of course, but Manolo planted himself bravely in front of my mother and father and said, "Look, Papá, it's no use, we want to be toreros, and that's all there is to it."

"Toreros!" my mother gasped, with the same tone she would have reserved for the word "burglars."

"Watching men risk their lives with bulls is one thing," said my father, "but wanting to do it yourselves is suicidal madness. We'll enroll you in Secondary One on Regina Street tomorrow!"

Two months later we were ushered out of there.

Confronted by such stubbornness, my father made us a

proposition: because of a whim (as he considered our project) he didn't want us to "become a couple of donkeys with no preparation for the battle of life." Therefore he would give us permission to study and practice bullfighting all day in exchange for going to night school. We accepted delightedly. But now how in the world did one set about becoming one of those splendid matadors we had admired so much?

"Go to the Tupinamba," a customer of my father's advised us. "That's where the bull folk hang out."

The Tupinamba, Calle Bolívar 44, is still the hub of the bullfighting world in Mexico City. It is a colorless, stark café where men sit for hours over a bun and coffee and discuss their own and other men's destinies.°

There they told us that one Don José Romero, "Frascuelillo," taught beginners and even had real bullfighting uniforms for rent, in case we wanted to dress up in them.

In case we wanted to dress up in them! This suddenly seemed the most important thing — much more so than actually learning how to fight. At the risk of a few small thefts from the tin in the kitchen that contained my mother's expense money we rented two complete uniforms from Don José, and then went and had ourselves photographed. When we saw the photo, nothing could possibly convince us that we were anything less than Gaona and Belmonte.

Don José showed us the first steps of "living room" bullfighting too and we practiced hard, using a blanket for a cape.

Toreo de salón is to a torero what shadow boxing is to a boxer, and all fighters practice the different passes assidu-

° James M. Cain's opening chapter in *Serenade* is the best description of what goes on in the Tupinamba. It starts out: "The place was pretty full, with bullfight managers, agents, newspapermen, pimps, cops, and almost everybody you can think of, except somebody you would trust with your watch."

Resplendent in the rented costumes.

ously with imaginary bulls in between encounters with real
ones. This much we knew.

But after a week we couldn't see how this was getting us
any closer to fighting an actual animal. Then we found out
that Samuel Solís, a fine ex-matador, had a bullfighting school
in the old plaza of Tacuba. We found out where he lived
and lay in wait for him one morning.

"Matador," Manolo started, tipping his hat to the well-dressed little man, "we are very fine toreros and we would like to join your school."

The man's kindly face wrinkled into a smile. "Aren't you a little young?"

"Oh no," I said and produced the photograph of us resplendent in the rented costumes.

He studied the photo gravely. "One can see you are great toreros," he said. "There is, however, a widespread belief that the intricacies of donning the suit of lights is one of the easier parts of a torero's performance." He gave back the photo, and patted me on the head. "Come around in a few years."

Manolo and I looked at each other in desperation as we watched our one chance walk away from us. Then suddenly Manolo nudged me, took off his jacket and ran down the street ahead of Maestro Solís. Kneeling down on the sidewalk he swirled out his coat in front of him the way he had seen Armillita do it. "Ah-hah, toro!" he called, shaking the jacket out with one hand, and I took my cue. Holding two forefingers to my head, I crouched over and charged. As I bore down on my brother, he swung the coat over his head and I roared by, making the swooshing noise I had heard the bulls make as they expelled air in the charges. I swung around and started to charge again and then I caught a glimpse of the Maestro's face. He was shaking his head grimly.

"You are dead," he said to Manolo. "Stone dead with a horn through your left eye. Don't you know the first thing about a larga cambiada? If the bull is charging from the right like that how in the world do you expect it to —" He sighed exasperatedly and rolled his eyes. "Good God, come to the school at ten. We must at least correct that."

We hugged ourselves with excitement and set off for the

school. And what a wonderful school it was. Our new companions received us warmly in spite of our age. They were a group of young fellows all full of dreams of glory and bound together by a consuming common interest. Some of us would be killed and others crippled before we could reach our goals, but right now the world was our oyster and we were invulnerable; we were positive it would always be "the other fellow" who would get gored.

The fellow I liked the best was an older boy about to graduate named Javier Cerrillo. A few years later he became and remained my right-hand banderillero until the day I "cut the pigtail," but now he was the king of the pupils because he had actually fought a few small bulls, and when he shook my hand warmly and exclaimed over the photo of Manolo and me, I felt an immediate affection for him that has never diminished. It was a lucky meeting for me, because he has saved my life several times, once in Colombia in the most unusual way imaginable — but that comes later.

A school of tauromachy much like the one run by Solís.

2

In Maestro Solís we had a fine teacher who really wanted to help us become adept at the profession he had loved and was too old to pursue.

The first thing he taught us was how to run and clear the bullring fence, using the estribo, the stirrup board which runs around the barrera a foot from the ground, as a take-off for the vaulting. He made us do this for hours, and it seemed a very undignified and unworthy thing for future fenómenos to start out with.

"Maestro," I said once accusingly, "you have told us that a matador never runs."

The man's eyes twinkled. "Ah, that is true," he said gravely. Then he winked. "But he knows *how* to run!" And he continued to make us practice our vaulting. The fence was higher than we were and it was many days before we could get over it without spilling headfirst into the alleyway. The Maestro would demonstrate for us, and with what ease that old man would run up to the fence, place his hands on the top board, take off from the estribo board, and sail over with his feet together gracefully. I call him an old man, for so he seemed to us, but actually he took his alternative from Belmonte in 1913, so he must have been under fifty at this time.

(When a bullfighter takes *la alternativa* he graduates from a novillero to a full matador, the goal of all us young toreros. We weren't even novilleros yet! Novilleros are not amateurs; they are professional apprentices, equivalent to preliminary boxers as opposed to main-eventers.)

Then came days of learning how to hold ourselves in the ring, how to walk, even how to parade into the ring with our left arms slung in a dress cape, how to bow to the presidente, and all the rest of the ritual. We put up with all this impatiently, wondering when the devil we were going to get down to brass tacks. I didn't realize still how very much there was to learn and how much groundwork and even history and the meaning of la fiesta brava's centuries-old ritual we were absorbing every day.

Finally the Maestro broke out the big capotes — the work capes — and there was great excitement. One after another he singled us out to perform our conception of a verónica.

"The verónica was named after the woman who held out a cloth to Christ," said the Maestro, "and it is at once the easiest and most difficult pass in bullfighting."

Anyone can do it badly, he explained, for it consists simply of holding the cape in both hands and swinging it in front of the bull's nose as he charges. Yet when done by an artist who knows how to use his wrists and his body to charge the maneuver with emotion, it can be the most exciting and graceful of all. He told us that the finest verónicas have been executed by Joselito, Gitanillo de Triana, and Solórzano.

When it was my turn I grabbed the cape confidently. My first surprise was at the weight of the cloth. I had been used to makeshift, homemade things, and I was not prepared for the heaviness of it.

The classic verónica
as executed by:

Joselito,

Solórzano

and Gitanillo,

Made of percale and silk, a capote is magenta-colored on the outside and yellow on the inside. It must be well made to withstand the beating it takes from the horns, and a good capote is worth around $60.

Striding out to the center of the little arena arrogantly, I chanted "Uh-huh, toro" at an imaginary bull and then swung the cape. I executed what I considered four superb verónicas worthy of Gaona himself, ended with my version of a half-verónica, and then strode away regally from my baffled bull. I expected a roar of applause, but all I got were a few snickers, and I saw the Maestro shake his head.

"Carlitos, have you got curvature of the spine?" he asked solicitously.

Crushed, I assured him I was in good physical shape. "Then wherever did you get that peculiar stance?" he said.

He took me over to the fence and pushed me back against the boards until my shoulder blades were flat against them. Then he made me swing the cape back and forth, back and forth, never letting any daylight show between my spine and the fence.

After a half-hour of this my arms were ready to drop off. But he kept me at it. The next morning I was so stiff Manolo had to tie my shoelaces for me. But back I went. Day after day I spent up against that fence, my wrists aching, my arm muscles screaming. Then he let me try it away from the fence. The first passes I made straight as a ramrod, but then on the last one I followed my natural tendency and bent from the waist. Back to the fence!

I finally mastered this phase of the verónica. Then he began working on my arm action, standing behind me and swinging my arms for me like a golf pro, teaching me to put my whole body behind the pass. I kept begging the Maestro to let me go on to other passes, but he wouldn't hear of it.

Manolo was much better at the verónica than I, and so

were the other boys. It was not Maestro Solís' fault; it was simply that I had no feeling for the pass. It was and has always been the weakest part of my performance.*

Finally we graduated to the fancy passes which are used for the *quites,* and I was much happier.

Quites, the Maestro explained, comes from the word *quitar,* meaning "to take away from," and refers to the man's luring the bull away from the picador's horse. The bull must charge the horses three times, and each time the matadors take turns caping the animal away. The first man will do a pass, and then the next man will try to outdo it in grace and daring, and the third man will try to "give the bath" to them both.

I seemed to have much more feeling for these flashy chicuelinas, where you spun gracefully in toward the bull's neck, or the gaoneras, where you arrogantly flipped the cape behind you, or the faroles and tapitías, where you pivoted around and around like a lighthouse. Even the Maestro seemed pleased. I was eager and impatient to get to the banderillas, the next phase, but now the Maestro introduced a new element: the bull. Well, not really a bull. Just a young man holding a pair of slaughterhouse horns, but he was trained to imitate a bull's reactions exactly. He would play fair and do nothing that a true fighting bull would not do. But just let us make a mistake, and he would drive into us with relish, and many times we had our skin punctured by those horns. "This boy weighs one hundred pounds," said our maestro. "The bull will weigh a thousand. So it will do a bit more than puncture the skin. Better get all the

* The ex-matador Chucho Solórzano said recently, "It's the only thing in the arena that Arruza doesn't do superbly. He stands straight enough, God knows, and works in as close to the horns as a man can, but he seems to disdain the bull, to act as though it isn't really there, which is fine for other passes but not for the verónica. 'Go *with* the bull, man,' I tell him, 'go *with* the horns with your whole body!' But this is a blind spot for him."

mistakes you can get out of your systems here."

It took many sessions to adapt the passes we had learned to the charges of the "bull." There was more to it now than just trying to look pretty. Where before we could simply make up our own rhythm as we wanted, now we had to be guided by the speed of the bull. If we swung the cape too slowly he stepped on it, jerked it from our hands, and jabbed a horn into our stomachs. If we swung too fast, we removed the lure from the attacker's vision, and he had every right to horn us, which privilege he exercised with pleasure.

After months with the intricacies of the cape, we went on to the second act of the corrida. From the very start, from the very first pair I had seen Armillita place, I was excited by the *palitroques*,* as the Maestro called them.

For this part of the training the carretilla — the mechanical bull — was used. This consisted merely of a stuffed bull's head mounted on a bicycle wheel and two long bars extending back for handles. A boy trained for it can simulate the charge of a bull perfectly with this contraption, and somehow for banderillas it really gives the sensation of an attacking bull much more than just a pair of horns does.

I remember the first morning of work on the banderillas. I listened impatiently as the Maestro said, "Here is the way banderillas are placed." He started to outline the theory of them, but before he'd delivered more than two sentences, I impetuously grabbed a pair of the sticks and ran out to the center of the ring. "Ah-ha, toro!" I yelled with supreme confidence. When the boy pushing the mechanical bull started toward me I loped calmly out at an angle. Then I doubled back fast, instinctively gauging the distance and the angle of the attacker so that when we came together in the center

---

* Slang word for the 26-inch sticks with the barbed points called "banderillas." Three pair are placed in every bull to further weaken the neck muscles of the animal so that he can be killed in the final act of the fight.

Now we had to be guided by the speed of "the bull."

of the ring, his momentum carrying him one way and mine carrying me the other made it impossible for the horns to snag me. I raised my arms as high as I could, planted the barbs in the chunk of cork behind the bull's head, let the horns graze by my rib cage, and then spun away and trotted to the fence.

There was a silence as I came back to the group, and I expected, and deserved, a severe scolding for my insubordination. But the Maestro simply turned to the other boys and said quietly, "Gentlemen, that is the way banderillas are placed."

Naturally I had a swelled head, but I couldn't take all the credit, because right from the start I had a natural God-given feeling for the sticks. My stock with the rest of the class, especially low since my backwardness in verónicas, went up, but then after a while we graduated to the third phase of the fight, the muleta and sword.

The muleta is the small red flannel cape used in the last part of the fight. A short stick (palillo) is fixed into it with a screw eye, and that is used as a handle to manipulate it. Where the big capote is essentially a two-handed cape, the muleta is essentially one-handed, either right or left, depending upon the pass.

Now work really began in earnest, for the maestro showed us how this is the most difficult and dangerous part of the fight. The bull at this stage is a much more wary and tricky animal than when he first came into the arena; after all, he'd never really encounted a dismounted man before, and throughout the fight he has learned a great deal. Also, the man is not hiding behind a big cape, nor is he running as when he places banderillas. He is standing still and holding the much smaller cloth away from his unprotected body. There was a whole new set of passes to learn, the natural with the right hand, the natural with the left, the chest pass, the statuesque passes, the punishing passes, the horn-to-horn passes, the flashy windmill passes and many more.

But more important even than the physical maneuvers were the lessons in bull psychology that Maestro Solís would give us. Sitting on the arena sand around him we would listen as he tried to teach us how a bull thinks. The obvious things we already knew, such as the basic fact that you should always keep your back to the fence when citing a bull to charge, since the average bull, when close to the barrera, tends to swerve away from the fence when it charges; therefore trying to make the bull pass between oneself and the boards is highly risky, since it might swerve into one without even meaning to.

However, Maestro Solís explained how some bulls behave exactly the opposite to the rule and tend to swerve *into* the fence! He told us how to spot those tendencies quickly and then how to fight them. He explained about the intricacies of querencias. During the progress of the corrida, bulls on the defensive often take preferences for certain parts of the arena. It might be completely arbitrary, or perhaps the spot where they have tossed a man or a horse and feel victorious; or close to the toril gate, where they first came in and feel secure. This place, or sometimes places, is called *la querencia,* he told us, and warned us that in it the bull will fight a dangerous, choppy, come-in-and-get-me type of fight, which is ruinous for any torero who is trying to show off his repertory of passes. The bull must be lured out of his querencia to another part of the ring; a bull with a strong urge to return to his querencia generally will charge best if placed in the center of the ring. A bull charging in the direction of his querencia will "pass" better than going the other way. When the bull makes a sudden charge to return to his querencia, and the bullfighter, realizing the bull is thinking more of where it's going than it is of hooking anybody, stands and makes some showy passes, it is called "taking advantage of the trip."

"It impresses only the greenest of aficionados and the tourists," the Maestro said.

Whereas I never could be bothered to learn geometry theorems, how I committed to memory every theory Maestro Solís offered! I would lie awake at night going over and over the strategems and techniques the Maestro had outlined.

The Maestro would take a puntilla, the coup de grâce dagger, and sketch out on the sand aerial views of a man and a bull to explain about the different terrains relating to the man's position to the animal and how it affected the subsequent charge and the bull's inclination to hook and swerve. I remember his lecture on bulls that are *tardos* — reluctant to charge — and how he told us to take a little step forward, while shaking the muleta and shouting at the bull to make it charge. "If it doesn't charge, take another step forward, again not toward it, but in front of it, as though to cross the line of its intended charge. But — " and then he pointed to the near horn of the sketch of the bull and extended it with a series of diagrammatical dots to the bullfighter, supposedly about ten feet away, "never cross this imaginary line or —" He smiled grimly and drew the dagger across his throat.

This was the theory in bullfighting then, and I, like everyone else, accepted it completely. You could not cross the intended line of a bull's charge, and that was all there was to it. A decade later Manolete was to show all of us how wrong we were. It merely took one man of extraordinary guts to try to prove you could get away with it. It was like Columbus — once he had the nerve to prove that ships weren't going to fall off a shelf into infinity, it was easy for the rest to follow. But I'm getting ahead of myself, for I wasn't to discover this revolutionary principle and then add my own contribution to the revolution for ten years.

Finally we came to the phase of killing. Again we used the mechanical bull, which had a small opening between its "withers." We were taught how "it's the left hand that kills, not the right." True, the sword is in the right, but it is the left that swings the muleta, keeps the bull's head down while the matador reaches over that right horn to plunge the sword in. It was like rubbing one's head and patting one's stomach. The Maestro kept telling us that it was just a pase de pecho — the across-the-chest pass which we had already learned — plus a sword thrust, but it was terribly hard to remember to swing the muleta in the left hand in front of the bull's nose while at the same time trying to hit that very small opening between the animal's shoulder blades. If we did move the muleta wrong, or stop it altogether, the "bull" would jerk up its head and we would be jabbed in the stomach or chest.

Now it was Manolo's turn to shine, for he was clearly the

best in the class at this killing business. He not only would hit the wire-meshed hole every time and swing his muleta perfectly, but he also had an elegance of style about the whole maneuver which I have never seen duplicated.

The Maestro even taught us how to take triumphant laps around the ring, holding up the ear of the dead bull and skimming back the hats the men tossed down and keeping the carnations that the beautiful women would surely throw to us. "Remember," said the Maestro, "in Mexico you take your laps counterclockwise — but when you get to Spain, you will go clockwise."

Spain! This was an impossibility, a wild, wonderful, impossible dream. Would any of us ever actually be good enough to fight in the mecca of bullfighting? Manolo and I didn't even dare talk about attaining such heights, but as we worked away at our strange apprenticeship, this is what was in the back of our minds always.

That whole year we didn't miss a single day of classes, our five senses concentrating on learning everything Don Samuel could teach us, and with the determination to become toreros or die in the attempt. Since we didn't go to school (and I refer to the other school, the boring one) until seven in the evening, in the afternoons we used to show my father in the tailor shop how handsomely we could bullfight. We would spend hours giving gaoneras and naturals before my poor papá, who felt he had to act like a father and be disapproving. He pretended he wasn't a bit interested, but I noticed that if Manolo or I were trying to execute some tricky maneuver his shears would stop snipping and he would watch the action out of the corner of his eyes. In spite of his telling my mother how he disapproved of all this, he was actually living all of our excitements with us and was secretly delighted.

One wonderful morning someone told us that an associa-

tion of hardware dealers was having a fiesta featuring *un
festival* — a small fight with minor matadors and small bulls.
Manolo and I looked at each other.

"What do you think?"

"Count on me."

We didn't have to say another word: we would fight our
first bull — we would be espontáneos!

An espontáneo is an amateur who jumps down in the ring
during a regular performance, capes the bull, and hopes to
attract the attention of a promoter. It is against the law,
and the usual punishment is fifteen days in jail. But so great
was our determination that we were ready to risk anything
— fifteen days was a small price to pay for a chance with
a real bull.

I hid a folded cape under my sweater, and Manolo tucked
a muleta and sword under his jacket. We paid our admission
for cheap seats high up on the sunny, inexpensive side and
prayed that none of the authorities would notice our strange
bulges. Halfway through the second bull Manolo whispered
to me, "You could do better with the cape than that matador!" I stared down at the black animal, a young novillo
that was little more than a calf but which suddenly looked
like the Insurgentes bus to me. "So could you," I said tensely.

"Well," Manolo said, "go down and prove it to them." He
was perspiring as much as I. "You go down!" I said. Neither
of us said anything. Then Manolo said, "Let's both go."

We shook hands. We sneaked our way down, squeezing
through the crowd, who immediately knew what we were
up to and made way for us, delightedly shielding us from
the sight of the ushers and other authorities. When we saw
the matador withdraw about twenty feet from the bull,
Manolo nudged me and we leaped down from the stands
into the passageway. The other toreros saw us and tried to
catch us before we got over the high fence, but Maestro

Solís' vaulting lessons came to our rescue and we cleared the barrera easily. As we ran out toward the bull we pulled out our capes. I got my capote ready first and was closest to the bull, so I ran up to it shouting, "Toro — ah-haaaa!"

As I watched the bull wheel and start to charge, the horrible thought struck me: this was not a friend of mine pushing a mechanical bull — this was a real and vicious wild beast that was charging to kill me. I froze for a fraction of a second. My first reaction was, God, he's going at this cape, so if I clutch it to me he won't see it and then he'll go away and leave me alone! That would have been fatal, of course, as the bull, following the movement of the cape, would have crashed straight into me. My next reaction was, God, he's going at the cape, so if I fling it from me he'll attack it and leave me alone! And as I watched the animal bear down on me I thought, Mother, help me, this idea of being a bullfighter was complete insanity! Mother!*

But so intense had been my training that my natural reactions were nullified — like those of a well-trained soldier going into combat for the first time. Instinctively, fighting my impulses, I held the cape out properly for the bull and made myself stand straight and as gracefully as possible, as though Maestro Solís were watching to see if I were keeping my back flat against that fence. Then as the horns came almost to my body I somehow swung the cape in front of the animal's nose and guided him past me, the horns just a foot or so away from my legs.

Later I learned that the crowd yelled "Olé!" but I was too absorbed in what I was doing to hear anything. So it worked! It actually worked the way the Maestro said it would. The bull went by without hitting me!

On the return charge I grew bolder. I flipped the cape

---

* Like Pierre in *War and Peace*, who looks at the enemy forces bearing down on him and thinks absurdly: "Can they be coming at me? And why? To kill me? *Me* — of whom everyone is so fond?"

around behind my back and did a fancy gaonera. Then another, and another, trying to work closer and closer and make each one more graceful. Now it wasn't so much different from the mechanical bull, except that the bulk of the animal's shoulder gave a different sensation as it went by, and also the real bull made a swooshing sound as it expelled its breath and seemed to charge faster than what I was used to. But how much more thrilling it was with a real animal! More exciting even than I had dreamed. What a sense of beauty and power, both at the same time, to control this deadly animal and do it gracefully!

I guess I must have done five or six gaoneras out there before I finally ended the series with a serpentina that swirled and blossomed out around my waist. Then I turned my back on the winded animal and strode away. I took a deep breath, the first since I'd taken on the animal. I suddenly heard the crowd cheering for the first time and that was very sweet too, though nothing compared to the exciting secrets the bull and I had just shared together.

The regular bullfighters grabbed me angrily as soon as I was far enough away from the bull. But now Manolo had his muleta in his hand and he was out there with the animal, making it charge at the red rag draped over the sword. He was always good with the muleta in practice and now he was doing everything that Maestro Solís had shown him. The bull was a perfect one — we didn't realize for a long time just how brave and easy-to-handle a bull we'd been lucky enough to encounter — and Manolo rose to the occasion. The crowd was applauding his every graceful pass. But then he withdrew from the animal for a breather, and in a second the other bullfighters had grabbed him. We struggled, but they began to hustle us out of the ring to jail. Whereupon the crowd arose as if one person, demanding that we be allowed to fight more! It was an

Arruza's first encounter with a live bull.

Manolo Arruza
killing his first bull.

amazing thing, but the toreros had to give in. So after each of us had made a few more passes, Manolo and I found ourselves in the middle of the ring flipping a coin to see which of us would kill the bull. Manolo won, and after lining up the bull the way we'd been taught, with its two front feet together to open up the shoulder blades, he sighted down the curved sword, flung himself straight over the bull's right horn, "crossed" perfectly with his left hand as the bull charged, and sank the blade up to the hilt in the animal. To mine, the crowd's, and Manolo's astonishment, at the end of that charge it slid to its knees, stone dead.

The crowd went wild. They threw hats and even money down to us, and we had to take several laps around the ring. We were delirious and everyone else was pleased too, with the exception of the professional toreros, who would have liked to see us in jail where they figured we belonged.

You can imagine our pride when we went to the real bullfight that afternoon. The big plaza de toros, El Toreo, seemed small, so enormous did we feel ourselves to be. A great aficionado whom we had met in the children's clothing shop my mother owned, took us to the fight and he introduced us to several of his friends as "those two phenomenons" who had fought that morning in the festival. What indescribable pleasure we felt when some of the people who had been in the festival called to us, "Enhorabuenas" — congratulations — just as though we were toreros. Well, that's all there was to it. We were playing for keeps now, and we *were* toreros!

Or so we thought, anyway.

The following morning a friend of Papá's dropped by to talk to him. He had been to the fight, and he gave a blow by blow description of our feats. Since he ran on so extravagantly, Papá went immediately over to see our teacher Solís in order to find out the true story. Don Samuel "ran the bull" for us so well that my father became really excited at our prospects. Now we had another ally in the fight against the displeasure of my mother, who never could be won over (and I don't believe any mother ever will be convinced about the merits of bullfighting, as far as her sons are concerned.)

The next step was that Javier Cerrillo, who was now a real torero, organized a corrida in Tula in Hidalgo, where he was appearing on the program with the lady bullfighter La Finita. He put Manolo and me in the cuadrilla of Finita as helpers. Things turned out fine for us, since we placed banderillas well and they allowed us to go out with the cape and we made a few pretty good passes in the *quites,* considering our inexperience. Things were not as good in the economic department. After the fight, Cerrillo came up to me and said rather imperiously, "Well, here's your salary," and handed me two and a half pesos.

It wasn't exactly Isabella's treasury, but money had never clinked more beautifully in a pocket, and I remember with affection the fact that Cerrillo was my first impresario, even though, just between us, I think he could have paid me a little more money. But afterwards, with his faithful friendship, he paid me back with interest, more than if he had given me a million pesos in Tula.

With the bullfighting fever burning stronger every day in our bodies, there finally arrived the longed-for moment of dressing ourselves in the traje de luces for our first real corrida. It was the 14th of November in 1934. The program was Pepe Estrada, my brother Manolo, and I, with six young bulls from Zacatepec. I had made a few passes at steers in the slaughterhouse, we had fought the small bull in the fight where we jumped down out of the stands, and then the business in Tula, but I had never gone out dressed in the real costume nor, much less, killed a bull.

At one in the afternoon I was already dressed like a bullfighter in my rented suit of lights, and was practicing passes all over the house in front of the terrified eyes of my mother, who had had a big quarrel with my father, since she never thought that matters would come to such an extreme. If it had been up to me, I'd have gone to the corrals for the drawing dressed in my gaudy uniform. Luckily, they didn't let me.

The bullfight began at four and never had hours seemed so long. Finally we set out for the plaza de toros. The arena of Vista Alegre had a tragic pall hanging over it. Two Sundays before, a bull had killed an unfortunate novillero named Miguel Gutierrez, and just before that an espontáneo, who had jumped down out of the stands like us, had also been killed. But here we were going blithely, my brother and I, with our hearts and our heads full of grandiose imaginary faenas.*

"When my first comes out," we said, "I'm going to do

* The faena is the last third of the fight; all the work with the muleta.

this and that and the other thing, and then you come out and do that *quite* that you've been practicing so much, and then I'll do the statuesque passes," and so forth and so on. The Maestro and my father were scared stiff. Manolo and I were completely calm, or rather so completely ignorant of what a truly terrible thing bullfighting can be that we didn't know enough to be scared; we didn't realize just how lucky we had been up to now as far as bulls went.

How did it turn out for us? Our luck with the bulls continued to be fantastic.

That afternoon in the arena of Vista Alegre, we carried off all our imaginary faenas. We did everything just about the way we had dreamed. All that we'd done in my father's tailor shop we repeated right in front of that threatening crescent moon of horns of the bulls.

We actually cried with emotion and joy when the crowd carried us around and around the ring in triumph. We were on our way now, and it hadn't been difficult. It was easy.

How quickly we were to learn the tough taurine facts of life!

That afternoon we carried off all our imaginary faenas.

CARLITOS
ARRUZA

3

THAT'S THE WAY our formal "debut" went — everything easy, everything just a splendid game.

The next day's dawn found my brother and me still talking about our prowess — after having chattered all night. The congratulations that we received from our companions the next day were many and sincere.

"To-re-ros!" They hailed us with the traditional chant given victorious matadors. There was no jealousy. They all were delighted and helped us start training, since we were fighting again on the coming Sunday. They argued among themselves as to who would have the privilege of acting as bull for us to practice with. What a fine time of my life that was.

Once again we yearned for it to be Sunday. When Manolo and I would walk home, it was always as though we were making the parade across the arena, our arms slung in imaginary dress capes. We would perform a verónica, a natural, a sword thrust on every tree that we passed. People in the street thought we were crazy, but we didn't see people anymore — we saw only audiences, jammed in our imaginary plaza, eager to applaud anything we did with those bulls that for the moment happened to be disguised as other objects. Bicycles, cars, bulls, we could handle anything.

Finally the week passed and once again we dressed as bullfighters. But now we didn't have quite that same wonderful unawareness of the Sunday before. Now we had the burden of having to justify last week's success. That was our big worry, and proves what I've always said: a successful afternoon is simply one that you've got to top the next time. That's how the never-ending chain starts, and once started one's tranquility is gone forever. And if you have a bad afternoon, that of course is worse, since the following performance has to be great to erase the bad odor. Therefore, in a torero's life the only really fine afternoon is the first one, since he doesn't have to worry about justifying any triumphs or obliterating any flops. But from that day on until the day he cuts off the pigtail, good-bye peace of mind!

As we drove to the plaza for this fight I was terribly worried. I noticed my brother was equally nervous. The roles were turned around now. Manolo and I didn't utter a word, whereas my father and Maestro Solís chattered like two magpies.

"We'll see another great afternoon today."

"Beginning of two highly promising careers."

They went on about how we couldn't fail to have another success, that once launched like this nothing could stop us, and so forth. Instead of calming us down it seemed to put even more responsibility on our shoulders and make the task ahead even harder.

Once in the plaza we managed to do well enough, but this time we knew a little more what we were doing. It meant more to us than the time before, because it showed our first performance wasn't all luck. I did all right with the cape and banderillas but I was terrible with the sword, which spoiled everything.

The next day I was very upset in spite of what everyone called a good performance. I wanted to fight again immediately to show everyone I *could* kill well. See — that peace of mind was gone and gone forever. My friends tried to cheer me up, saying it could happen to anybody, even to the big stars, but I felt I had been like the fox who drew the pretty pictures in the sand, and rubbed them out with his tail.

I spent weeks then doing nothing but killing the mechanical bull, flinging myself over that right horn hour after hour, trying to hit the vital spot, the small opening of the pipe. After the other students had gone home I'd still be there making sword thrust after sword thrust, until it was too dark to see or until my fingers could no longer close around the red hilt of the sword. Then I would go home and study books about bullfighting to get some glimmer of their techniques. Once I saw an old engraving of a bullfighter resting his elbow on a bull's forehead after a pass, and though I dismissed it as impossible, I never forgot it. Ten years later it was to come in handy.

Then one day Maestro Solís said I'd get a chance to redeem myself and to pack my things, for we were off to Morelia. Our first trip! We were big-shot toreros now — at the ages of fourteen and fifteen, respectively. As we rode along in the train (an exciting thing in itself since it was our first), we imagined the big crowds that would be there to greet the Arruza brothers and to carry us through the streets to our hotel. We distinctly heard the cries of "Here are the stars of Mexico City — the new fenómenos of the bull world!"

There not only wasn't a crowd at the station, there wasn't

anyone. The next day we began our publicity campaign. This consisted of dressing up in the bolero jackets and broad-brimmed hats of the traje corto costume of the type that Joselito and Belmonte used to wear. They were made for us by our father and we thought we were just about the nattiest pair of toreros in the world. I do remember that my shirt was a little too large and that my brother had to wedge a chewing gum package between my collar and neck to make it look right. I had to walk very stiffly so that it didn't slip down my back, and I heard someone whisper, "My, how regally he walks for a child." Later, when a group of toughs called us sissies and beat us up, we decided to abandon this dress.

Although the fight on Sunday went wonderfully in all other departments, I again was terrible with the sword. I just couldn't kill the animal.

"It's made of concrete," I gasped to Manolo.

I tried and tried, tears of frustration running down my face. Finally I heard the terrible warning trumpet which meant that very shortly the bull would be led out alive, the worst disgrace of all for a torero. However, before the final trumpet the poor bull died, more out of boredom than anything else, I'm afraid.

But how my brother killed that day! How I admired and envied his style and skill. My ambition was to be just like him.

In spite of my shortcomings we were booked in Mexico City again, and it was there that I was awarded my first ear. What a great thrill it was to see the sea of white handkerchiefs waved by the crowd, hear them shout, "Oreja, oreja!" and then have the presidente accede to their wishes and grant me the ear off the young bull. Just a bloody, hairy piece of gristle that wouldn't bring two cents, but as I took my triumphal laps around the ring holding it up

I wouldn't have traded it for the Hope diamond. With great pride I handed it to my father over the barrera, and I saw he was moved beyond words. To make everything complete, Manolo was also awarded the ear off his bull.

This led to seven fights on seven consecutive Sundays in Guadalajara. Papá was forced to agree not to have us go to school, not because we'd convinced him, but simply because we had to stay in Guadalajara all that time. Nevertheless, he bought textbooks and every afternoon from four till six he would be the professor, teaching us grammar, geography, and arithmetic.

I don't believe my father ever had studied that much in

I was awarded my first ear.

his life before as he did trying to keep a lesson ahead of us. But I also must confess that though every class started with the highest intentions, it never was more than twenty minutes before he would interrupt a recital of the names of the capitals of the European countries to say something like "Carlitos, those banderillas al quiebro — just how is it that you make the animal veer off its course so as to avoid the horns?"

And then the session, like all of them, would completely disintegrate into an excited discussion of bullfights and we always ended up giving him lessons in the art of tauromachy. My poor father. Although we fought thirty-five "becerradas" — calf fights — that year and were artistic successes, we weren't making much money. He had to sell the business he had worked so hard for in order to back us and devote his time to managing us. Luckily my mother's shop for children's clothing was doing all right. She of course had never seen us fight, never would, and was still horrified that my father had reached the point of actually encouraging us. But once she saw the inevitable she accepted it and imbued us with that wonderful faith mothers have that everything would always turn out for the best.

4

DURING OUR TRIP we got the chance to actually meet some top matadors, stars like Alberto Balderas, Lorenzo Garza, Chucho Solórzano, and Heriberto García. Back in the city, we were drawn like filings to magnets to the "Tupi" and other cafés where these and the other demigods, the "real toreros," as we called them, might drop in. It was as though by inhaling the same air as they at close quarters we might absorb some of their skill. We began hanging around the cafés all afternoon every day, which pleased my parents not at all; one thing was to want to become toreros but turning into café bums was quite another. The only employment we had was helping Javier Cerrillo in his business; to make ends meet he made funeral wreaths and our job was to scan the newspapers and track down wealthy corpses whose families would be receptive to owning a genuine handmade Cerrillo floral wreath.

My mother suggested that instead of such highly diligent loafing, we might care to help her in the shop. So we accepted the jobs of delivering clothes, picking up materials, and other tasks totally unworthy of two great stars

Alberto
Balderas

of the taurine world such as the Arruza brothers. (Our real name was Ruiz-Camino but we took the maiden name of our grandmother for a *nom de taureau*.) My father also got the idea, mostly through my mother, that since we had time on our hands (it was the time of the *temporada formal* — when only full matadors were allowed to fight) it might be very nice for us to learn a more stable

Lorenzo
Garza

Chucho Solórzano

profession, namely, his. So he set us to learning how to be tailors. It was pathetic how happy it made my mother to see us doing something besides bullfighting. Although we were still going to the bullfighting school every morning she kept hoping that we would become so interested in being tailors that we would forget "all that other" as a childish whim. My father rather did, too, now, and tried to show us all the tricks of the craft.

"Maybe the bullfighting *was* crazy," he said, putting aside the dreams of glory and acting the sensible father. "This will please your mother very much."

He was in one of his brief conversative periods now. He had come to think of Monte Carlo as somewhat of a gamble, his latest oil-drilling venture had not yielded water — much less petroleum — and he had recently even turned down a sure-fire scheme for synthesizing diamonds. So we had to humor him and be industrious.

In our new apprenticeship we reached the stage of making a pair of tailored trousers, but when we got through with them they looked like two joined smokestacks. Another go at it, and this time the customer couldn't get his feet through them. How could we concentrate on the width of a pair of pants when running through our brains was how we would finish off that series of great gaoneras with the flashiest rebolera ever executed? Our chosen profession and the one chosen for us were as alike as an egg and a chestnut. Finally our parents had to admit it.

"All right," said my perfectionist father, resignedly, "You've convinced us that the tailoring profession would be imperiled if you dedicated yourselves to it. So — make yourselves into toreros and nothing but toreros. But be the best, or be nothing."

Once again, dread and worry for our mother and elation for us, because the novillada season was upon us again. By now my father had rid himself of his annoying sensible feelings of responsibility, and he threw himself jubilantly into this new kind of gambling — the gamble of the arena.

But the jubilation didn't last long. It took only one fight in the provinces to show that something was happening to me. I remember coming over to the fence after a series of what I thought were pretty good gaoneras.

"What's the matter?" I asked my father bewilderedly. "They're not applauding."

As with any prodigy the difficult time is bridging the gap between childhood and young manhood. The unconscious

Heriberto
García

grace people had admired the year before suddenly disappeared as I hit the gangling stage. I had had too much fundamental training to be really awful, but on the other hand nothing I did in the ring could ever have been called artistic or could have excited a crowd. I only got three fights all year. My father had gambled and lost again.

Finally he said sadly, "We'd better split you up."

We broke up the team and my brother did a little better than I on his own, but still we were both old-hat all of a sudden. From "young phenomenons" we had suddenly become "oh, *them!*"

We were getting no place. Then one day my father said, "We'll risk everything — we'll go straight to Spain!"

España — España!

Just to hear that word gave me chills. Every young torero dreams of Spain and triumphing there. My father's optimism, the unquenchable, unrealistic optimism of the confirmed gambler, was contagious, and we set off confidently.

We not only didn't triumph, we didn't even fight. It could not have been worse. The year was 1936. No sooner had we arrived in Spain than their terrible civil war broke out. "Just a little skirmish — question of days," my father said authoritatively. So we waited, and the booming of the cannons grew louder and closer. My father fell ill and we couldn't have left Madrid had we wanted to. He was so sick that he couldn't get out of our top-floor room even when the bombs were raining around us. At first, with the help of some neighbors, we tried to carry him out of that dangerous place down to one of the shelters, but his pain was so intense that he wouldn't let anyone touch him.

"Go — leave me!" he'd order when the raids would start. "Go down to the shelters!"

But we refused and stayed there cowering and praying during every bombing for a year. Food and money got scarcer and scarcer. My mother sent us as much money as she could every month but it wasn't enough. Finally it was decided that I should return to Mexico, since it was clear the war was going to go on and on, and my brother would return when my father was well enough to travel. But how to get there? I set off across the chaos that was Spain by any means I could find. I begged a ride on a troop truck and as we arrived in Aranjuez a great bombardment broke out. A bomb exploded near us, the truck crashed into a wall, and we were all spilled out into the street. So great still was my drive that I remember even in that second when I thought I might be killed I thought: Please don't let me die, Virgen mia, as I have so many bulls still to fight and I haven't even made a name for myself yet!

I was shaken up but was all right, and took a train jammed with refugees that day for Valencia. Somehow I managed to zigzag my way across Spain and France and finally arrived in Paris. I was completely broke and had lived on oranges for most of the trip, but I knew that once I got to the Mexican Embassy all would be well, because my mother was sending me money and steamship passage there. I walked all the way from the station to the Embassy because I only had nine francs and didn't know how much a taxi might be. When I arrived, ragged and exhausted but jubilant, in the elegant hall of the Embassy, the concierge looked at me with obvious distaste. I showed him my passport, made out in my real name, Carlos Ruiz-Camino.

"Please give me the money right away, as I'm starved," I said.

He checked. "Nothing for Ruiz-Camino," he said.

I was completely dumfounded. I didn't know what to do. I asked the concierge to keep my suitcase and the sheath I carried my swords in until my money arrived, which it surely would any moment.

That night I spent my nine francs on a good dinner, confident that I would be rich the next day. As for a place to sleep, I slept in the glassed-in portion of an open-air restaurant called the Café de La Tour, on a couple of benches. I also slept there the next night and for fourteen nights after that, because the money didn't arrive.

I stole fruit to live on and spent my days wandering desperately around the elegant streets of Paris and hanging around the Embassy waiting, waiting. I grew so desperately hungry that I finally pulled out a gold inlay from one tooth. All that pain for nothing, since nobody wanted to buy it after I had it out! Finally, in desperation I asked the concierge for my sword case, with the idea of hocking one of my beloved swords. As he handed it to me his eyes fell on the carved leather where it said: "Hermanos Arruza."

His mouth dropped open. "Your name's Arruza — not Ruiz-Camino?" He came back in a moment with the money that had arrived in Paris the day before I did. I was never so glad to see anything in my life. Unlike many unfortunate bullfighters who suffer years of hunger to arrive at the top, this was my one and only period of starvation, and that only because of a small mistake.

5

I RETURNED to Mexico and attempted to further my career, but with little success. My father returned, finally, still very ill, and Manolo and I both stormed the bastilles together.

Luck was completely against us. Our attempts to appear in the important bullrings, and above all in Mexico City, were intensified day after day. Nevertheless, we couldn't get any corridas. We made the rounds of all of the two-bit towns, but we never got a fight in a plaza of any importance at all. Taking the long view of it, perhaps this period of apprenticeship and struggle did us good. The bulls that we had to fight in those rings were discards, devilish bundles of tricks and craftiness that forced us to use every bit of resourcefulness and knowledge that we had to come out at all. Thus we had to learn how to fight really well before learning how to fight merely prettily. This, after all, is the main principle behind bullfighting.

We were approximately a year and a half making the whistle-stop circuits, until 1938, when I managed to fight two novilladas in Mexico City. I didn't attract any attention by my small-town style, which by now had become very ingrained in me. Though young still, I was already getting old in the profession without the slightest indication of my becoming a *figura* in the bull world. At barely eighteen years of age, I was already better known in all of the Republic than any of the other novilleros. These others, by their very newness, pleased the public more than I did.

My situation was precarious. I certainly wasn't going ahead in bullfighting, and on the other hand I didn't have any desire or aptitude to study or take up work of any other type. With my burning desire to bullfight I would have flopped at any other endeavor. In that period I got very little sleep worrying about what to do.

Once again the big bull season started and with it came complete inactivity. All we could do was to sit around our café in front of our banquets of coffee and bread and perform thrilling verbal bullfights to each other.

One day right in the midst of a great faena of mine, Manolo slapped his hand down on the table, "Portugal!"

"What?"

"We'll go to Portugal! There's no war on there and we'd be a novelty!"

"I hear the bulls are enormous and difficult."

"The Arruza brothers can handle any animals."

"All right — we'll go!"

We made the trip full of sadness. A few months before we had gone through the grief of losing our father, who could never get back on his feet after his illness. The poor man died leaving us disconsolate, since, aside from the great sorrow of losing a father, we had also lost our best ally, without really having been able to show him that all the faith he had had in us wasn't misplaced. He'd gambled and lost for the last time.

We arrived in Lisbon knowing absolutely no one.

"Now what do we do?" I asked Manolo as we wandered

around the strange city. "Here we are with no money and no contracts to fight."

"Someone told me all the bull people hang out around the Café Suizo. We'll see what's doing there."

On the way to the café we saw gaudy posters announcing that the coming Sunday there would be a corrida in which that marvelous Portuguese-style* bullfighter called Nuncio was going to take part along with two young Spanish no-villeros.

In the Café Suizo, a counterpart to our beloved Tupi-namba back home, we sat and elegantly drank coffee for hours, hoping to make contact with the people connected with bullfighting. Our wallets were well stocked with dozens of photos of us in action, and we passed them from table to table as calling cards, trying to look nonchalant, experienced, and highly successful. With the few pesos we still had we kept inviting people around us to join us in a *cafezinho*.

"This is getting expensive," I whispered to Manolo after paying for a round for a large group. "We don't have much left."

"We have to make a big impression," Manolo whispered back. "We have to show them who the Arruza brothers are."

No one seemed a bit impressed with the Arruza brothers, but they kept drinking off us.

And then we caught this bit of dialogue between two men at our table:

---

* "Portuguese style" refers to the art of rejoneo, where a man mounted on a superbly trained horse avoids the bull's charges while placing bander-illos and spears, called rejones. The object, completely the opposite from a picador's office, is to keep the horse from even getting scratched while the man shows off his horsemanship. The greatest exponents of this art have been Nuncio, Simao da Veiga, Cañero, Conchita Cintrón, Alvaro Domecq, and now Angel Peralta.

"Understand the impresario's stuck."

"So I gather. No toreros."

"Couldn't get visas — Spanish War."

We glanced at each other. We got up casually, said good-bye to our new acquaintances, strolled nonchalantly out of the café, and then streaked for the impresario's office. We got in to see him without too much trouble, and dumping our load of photos on his desk we said, "You have to put us on, señor, we will be great and make you a lot of money! Please put us on!"

He was a very decent man and he listened with great patience to the torrent. He studied the photos carefully. Then he sat back in his chair and said, "I don't doubt that you're very fine toreros, but I — and you must forgive my lack of awareness — I quite frankly have never heard of you. The plaza of Campo Pequenho, the greatest in Portugal, cannot risk introducing two, excuse the expression, two unknowns, so could you, if it wouldn't be too much bother, before I decide, could you just give me a little sample of the kind of toreros you are?"

We nodded numbly.

"Then be at the bullring in half an hour — and ready to perform."

Imagine how we left that office. Everything now was going to depend on what we might do with this bull that he was going to test us with. What ranch would it be from? Would it charge well? How big would it be? For thirty minutes we sweated. What a rough go it was, to fight like this without any warning and without being prepared or dressed right. On this was our whole future career to depend? We tried to cheer each other up, giving each other all kinds of advice and trying to plan how we'd work it. We decided that we would do it the way we did it when we were kids and first threw ourselves into the ring back in Mexico. "Manolo, you fight for a while and then I'll go out, and then we'll flip for who'll kill."

Finally, very fearful that things would not turn out well, we arrived at the bullring with its empty stands. "Ready?" the impresario said to us. "Ready, señor," Manolo said bravely, "whenever you please." We went into the ring. We prepared our capes and muleta, got ourselves into that who-cares-about-living-anyway frame of mind one needs just before a corrida, and then gave him the sign that we were ready.

"Let loose the bull!" I called.

"What bull?" asked the man.

Then we found out that our enemy was to be ourselves. All the impresario wanted to see was us fighting *de salón!* He explained to us that he just wished to see us swing the capes and go through the motions of placing banderillas. If we did it well, that was enough for him.

My God! And just for this we had gone through a half-hour of anguish!

At fighting *de salón* and at playing a brave fighting bull nobody in the world could beat us. We had behind us the wonderful experience of the bullfighting school of Solís, and you can't imagine the tremendous performances we put on, Manolo and I, that afternoon. When the bull is your brother, how can you lose?

"Well, señores," said the impresario afterwards. "You are quite splendid. I just hope the presence of rather large bulls won't dim the brilliance of your performances to-morrow."

That afternoon the whole Café Suizo knew that we were fighting the next day. The afternoon papers came out with our names announced on the program, the posters went up on the billboards shortly and the whole thing was getting so important it scared us. It had all happened so fast!

In the morning we went to see the bulls. They were not only the biggest animals we'd ever fought, they were the biggest we had ever seen. When we got there they had one of the monsters in a squeeze chute and they were preparing to saw off the points of the horns.

"Say, what are you doing?" Manolo called down to the men.

"This is Portugal," one answered. "No picadors. We always take the points off."

"These aren't your Mexican calves," said another. "And we'd hate to see young blood all over our pretty sand."

Then to my astonishment Manolo ordered, "Don't touch this animal's horns and don't touch any of the others!"

The men looked up at us. "Are you crazy?" But Manolo's tone made them put down the saw.

Manolo tried to look casual. "I don't believe in taking advantage of the animals."

The men snorted at this arrogance. "Sonny, you're going to wish to God we'd cut these babies' advantages off right close to the head before this afternoon's over! But if that's the way you want it, that's the way it'll be."

As we left I whispered to Manolo, "But they're cathedrals, those animals! What'd you go and do that for?"

"We've just got to be good, Carlitos," Manolo said, determined but a little pale. "Think how fine it will be if we get through this well."

"Think how fine it will be if we get through it at all," I answered.

"Look, buck up," he said. "We're the Arruza brothers!"

"That's right," I said gloomily. "I forgot — we can handle anything."

Word of our act — or rather Manolo's — spread like wildfire through the city, and now in the streets people began to look at us with a touch of respect. "Are they crazy?"

they asked. Yes, we were crazy. Crazy to do so well that we'd be another step closer to being full matadors instead of just unknown novilleros.

I was white when I saw my first bull of the afternoon slam out of the toril. It looked so terribly big and its horns were so sharp. Damn Manolo and his sportsmanship! I waited so long and let the banderillero cape it so much that the crowd began to catcall. "Where's the matador?" they demanded.

"Carlos, it's a dream bull!" said Manolo, shaking me. "Just act as though it were small — just do everything you'd do if it were a calf!"

I pulled myself together and went out there. It was a little hard to imagine that this animal whose shoulders were up to mine was a calf, but I kept saying to myself: "This is just a bull — a little bull like any other — and you can handle him, boy."

After two passes I saw that Manolo was right — the bull charged as though it were on rails and my confidence came rushing back to me; the size really didn't matter too much, if you put it out of your mind. I gave out with my entire repertoire and the crowd appreciated every pass much more than usual because they knew the bull had those sharp horns intact, something they'd never seen in Portugal.

My entire repertoire.

Naturally, without any picadors to slow the animal down, it was almost too much bull to handle, but the audience realized this and understood. At one point in the fight I wanted to leave the animal, to walk away and catch my breath after so many passes, but the bull wouldn't let me. He just kept charging and wheeling and charging and charging with this great power and strength. We stayed out there in the center of the ring, in the center of the world, in what seemed like one continual prolonged pass, the bull and I drunk with what we were doing.

Then suddenly — in the middle of a spinning molinete pass — I felt the animal's bulk swerving into me instead of hurtling on by. And then in the next instant I felt myself flung into the air. I felt the tip of the right horn jab into my flesh, but I grabbed the horn at the base and pushed myself off it and away from the bull's lethal head. When I hit the ground I was momentarily stunned. I saw the animal lunging at me again. Then the red flash of a cape came

I felt the tip of the right horn.

I was
momentarily
stunned.

between me and the horns and I realized that Manolo was luring the animal away. I scrambled to my feet and saw that I had a slight wound on my thigh. The sight of the blood running down my leg made me furious and I snatched up my muleta and went back to passing the bull closer than before.

In Portugal they don't kill the bulls, they only imitate the sword thrust using a banderilla, but they execute the maneuver in exactly the same way. I lined the bull up, profiled, and went through the motions of a perfect sword thrust, and that was the topper. The crowd was completely an insane asylum now, and they made me take lap after lap around the ring, me with a big lump in my throat. I neither saw nor felt anything, not even the wound in my leg. It was a great triumph. On my second bull the success came through the banderillas, which is one of the most popular acts of the bullfight in Portugal, and one with

Success came through the banderillas.

which the bullfighter who knows how to do it well can
perform all season on the strength of that alone. I placed
the banderillas so well that on this one bull they made me
place seven pairs instead of the usual three! The crowd
was a howling group of madmen. I will never forget that
afternoon, no matter how many years go by. These were
other faces, another type of public, other surroundings, and
there was frenzy in the stands. My brother also had a
complete triumph on one of his bulls, and the two of us took
laps around the ring together.

The reviews the next day were wonderful. My leg wasn't
hurt badly, and we were immediately contracted for the
following Sunday at a price that we never thought we'd
ever earn. It was an astronomic figure. (However, once
we had paid our expenses and translated their money into
our currency, we saw that it wasn't quite so much; but
any way you looked at it, it was more money than we ever

thought we'd see for just one bullfight.) The program for the coming Sunday was formed around us, and many a Sunday after that during the next two years. We returned to Mexico, but never with the luck that we had in Lisbon. My record of good fights there, more than anything I did in Mexico, finally put me in a position to "take the alternative" — to become a full matador — in 1940.

6

ALMOST SEVEN YEARS I had dreamed of *la alternativa* — when I would have served my long hard apprenticeship as a novillero and could rightfully use the title "Matador de Toros" and enter the ranks of the forty or so top toreros of the world who fought in the best plazas de toros against the finest bulls. I had been passed over by the impresarios for one reason or another for two years now, so when I finally received a telephone call from Dr. Gaona, the impresario of the Mexico City ring, asking if I'd be ready for the ceremony of becoming a senior matador the following week, I was almost unable to answer.

I spent those seven days like a sleepwalker. Matador de Toros! And I was to receive the title from the great Armillita, the first matador I had ever seen perform.

Things started off wrong when I almost didn't arrive at all at the plaza because of traffic. Then the crowd in the stands seemed very serious and hostile to me. Was there really any possible way of making those faces break into smiles or a cheer?

The great Paco Gorraez, who was to be witness to the

ceremony, arrived and then Armillita, and it all seemed unbelievable. I had a really handsome set of nerves built up now. What was I, Manolo Ruiz-Camino's little brother, doing here with these immortals of the bullring? I should be home helping my mother in the shop.

And when I heard the trumpet, I thought: Jesus, I'm not ready, this was too soon, give me a year or so more, I'm not ready to play with the big boys yet.

Then I swore at myself: All these years of work and now you're going to blow the big moment because of nerves?

The first bull came in, large, black, and well armed, with the number eleven branded on his side, from the fearsome ranch of Piedras Negras. The "alternative" ceremony made him mine, instead of belonging to one of the older matadors, as would normally be the case. I gritted my teeth and went out with the big cape. I was jumping all over the place with nervousness, couldn't get my feet to stay still, and didn't do anything worth looking at. I calmed down much more during the *quites,* worked in closer to the horns, and got some applause. I decided I'd better not place the sticks at all, and passed that job on to one of my banderilleros. Then came the ceremony, the solemn moment when Armillita came up to me out in the ring and handed me his sword and muleta. I was completely cool now and determined to give a great performance with the muleta.

Armillita said, "Good luck, boy. You are now a full matador, and with your talent the sky is the limit." Then he added a sentence that ruined everything. Very casually he looked over at the bull across the ring, shook his head, and said, "Watch that right side of his — he could be highly unpleasant with that right saber."

These words, spoken with honest intent to help me avoid an accident, were my downfall. Coming from the maestro

I felt more surprise than pain or terror.

of maestros to a neophyte who hadn't even particularly noticed any defect in the bull, they completely upset me. Instead of going out there with my usual happy, ignorant confidence, which I had always felt was the mother of safety, I went out bent on just one thing — to protect myself from that right horn where the maestro had seen so much danger lurking. When I looked at the bull now it seemed as though that damned antler fairly glowed with death!

And it turned out he was correct. As I finally flung myself on the animal to kill it, it jabbed viciously with its right and sank the horn up into my body. It was almost as though I had impaled myself on purpose so as not to make a liar out of the maestro. Except for the very slight wound in Portugal, this was my first real goring, and I think I felt more surprise than pain or terror when the horn slashed into my flesh like a baling hook. As I went up in the air my thoughts were more *Now the bastard's ruined my whole afternoon* rather than *God, maybe I'm being killed!*

The bull crashed over dead, but I was carried into the infirmary, crying with disappointment. Thus, what I had hoped would be my greatest day, ended in disaster.

After I had been operated upon and lay there in the infirmary in the depths of despair, the marvelous horn-wound specialist, Dr. Rojo de la Vega, read me the beginning of the medical report in an attempt to cheer me up.

"Matador de Toros, C. Arruza, entered the infirmary with a horn wound this afternoon, et cetera, et cetera. You

I was carried into the infirmary.

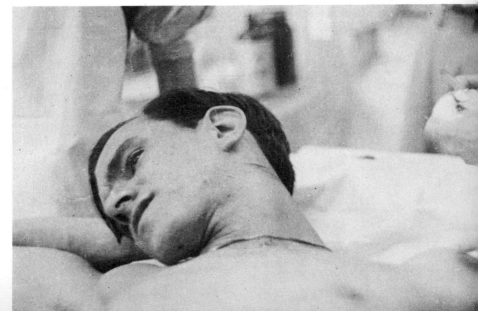

see, Carlos, it doesn't say 'novillero,' but rather 'Matador de Toros.' Try never to forget it, don't get discouraged, and always honor that title."

Gracias, Doctor!

I needed all the encouragement I could get. Of course my wonderful brother was always around when I needed him, and he helped me a great deal, even though he was going through a bad period himself and was very despondent. Because he'd been born in Madrid, the boycott between Spanish and Mexican toreros prevented him from fighting in Mexico and becoming a full matador. After the hospital, he threw himself into the hard task of getting me in shape again, worrying and wondering, as I was, if I still had my nerve, but feigning absolute confidence in me.

For some reason this was a bloody period in Mexican rings. Nearly every Sunday there was a goring. The week before I made my reappearance, Alberto Balderas, one of my boyhood idols, died with a bull's horn spiked through his chest. This shocked everyone in Mexico but especially the toreros who had fought side by side with him and

The death of Alberto Balderas on the horns of the Piedras Negras bull, "Cobijero," December 29, 1940.

revered him. And then not so long afterwards the twenty-year-old novillero star, Felix Guzmán was gored through the back and died three days later.

Maybe because of this I did badly on my reappearance. I was competing against such greats now as Garza and Chucho Solórzano and it was too much for me. I suddenly realized that my struggle was just beginning when I took the alternative, not ending or leveling off. I was no longer to be forgiven for mistakes or ineptness because I was young and an apprentice — the crowd paid money now to see an expert, and their demands were much greater. So were the demands of the bulls, now larger, older, and trickier.

In my next fight, with Carnicerito and Andrés Blando, I did a little better and was even accorded a sort of begrudged lap around the ring. But as I ran around the ring throwing back the few hats and flowers tossed down to me, a pretty blond tourist stood up and cried, "Here, handsome!" She threw down something white, and I, thinking it was a handkerchief, picked it up and waved it. It was a brassière.

The crowd burst into laughter. The few good things I'd done that day were forgotten. My reputation sagged to a new low. I was known in some circles as the "Brassière Kid" and suddenly found I couldn't get a fight anywhere in Mexico. Sunday after Sunday went by and I was the most unemployed torero around. I finally had to go to Venezuela to get fights. More bad luck: I was doing fine in my first corrida in Caracas, when the bull suddenly swerved and I got gored in my right hand.

Back in Mexico my bad luck got worse. First, my devoted manager, Benjamín Villanueva, died suddenly. Then the most terrible thing of my life happened: my brother was killed in a pistol accident. When this happened, the bottom dropped out from my world. I didn't want to live any more, struggle any more, triumph any more. Even now I cannot talk or write about it in detail.

My drive to be a great matador seemed to dribble away. After all, what was the thrill of cutting an ear if it wasn't Manolo's joyous face behind the barrera, and his jubilant claps on the back, and the long sessions at night at home reliving and refighting the whole corrida? I knew Manolo would want me to keep fighting, so I went on trying to become a good torero, but with no real spirit and no ambition. And hence no success.

I went to Portugal and had the most disastrous season of my life. Bad luck and my mental state combined to produce performances that were an insult to the good Portuguese people who had helped me so much in the earlier days. What little money I managed to make there I squandered. To get back to Mexico I had to borrow money from the Mexican Ambassador in Portugal.

Then followed two years of bad performances in Mexican rings, and worst of all in Mexico City, where without fail I consistently drew ugly and uncooperative bulls that I was incapable of handling.

I suppose I would have drifted on and on like this, unhappy in my mediocrity and not knowing quite what to do about it, if it hadn't been for a girl. She is a well-known actress now, so I'll call her Linda (Beautiful), because she certainly is that. I saw her first at a jai alai game one evening. One glance at her fresh young face, the alert dark eyes, the full lips that always seemed about to say something surprising, the long dark hair, the extraordinary figure, and my gaze never went back to the players. She was sitting one row away from me with another girl and a man, and I tried to hear her animated talk and catch every detail of her vivacious face.

I had never believed in love at first sight, but here I was with a heart going a mile a minute and sweat on my brow and I had never even spoken to the girl. Toreros, ugly or handsome, seem to have an allure for women by the very nature of their profession; I had had my share, beginning when I was fourteen. There was the handsome older woman in Guadalajara, the actress from Hollywood with the husband who was always, thank heaven, conveniently drunk, the cabaret girls, the cabinet minister's daughter, the wealthy rancher's sister, — the usual lot that falls to the average torero. Always it was brief and highly physical. I could get into the affair and out with no entanglements emotional, legal, or economic.

But Linda had a different effect upon me. I felt I would die to get to know, to possess this beautiful creature for always. I wanted to impress her in a dramatic fashion, so in a loud voice I made a fantastically large bet on the next game. It was nearly all the money I had in the world, and I did it very ostentatiously but without the slightest thought as to what I was betting on. When I won, I saw she was indeed impressed as I casually stuffed the money in my pocket. A few minutes later I screwed up my courage enough to talk to her; soon I deserted my friends to sit up next to her. She had a charming friendliness and openness and unaffected lack of coquettishness that was rare in a girl of barely eighteen, especially one so striking. I had the feeling she hadn't found out how truly attractive she was. In fifteen minutes I was completely and hopelessly in love for the first time in my life. She told me she was learning to be an actress and that someday she would be a big star. I didn't know much about acting, so I quickly got the conversation around to something I was an expert on: me. She said she liked bullfights and thought she had heard of me but wasn't sure.

"Do you know Manolete?" she asked eagerly.

I had to admit that I hadn't even seen the Spanish master who was considered the greatest of all matadors. Upon entering the jai alai court I had spotted a top Mexican matador whom I knew quite well, so when I suggested to Linda that we leave I made sure to steer her near where he was sitting.

"Oh there's Fulano de Tal!" Linda exclaimed. "I've seen him fight and he's marvelous."

"Like to meet him?" I said casually.

"Would I!"

I introduced them, and though she was very impressed, I think he was more so as he ran his eyes over her full young figure in the simple white dress.

We left and walked along the avenue, and Linda chatted happily about her dreams as though we'd known each other a long time. It seemed to me that never was a moon so big or a night so beautiful. We went to El Patio, an elegant and expensive restaurant. I had the money I'd won at the jai alai and I was out to impress this girl any way I could, so we had champagne and all the trimmings and she was impressed. There was an orchestra playing and Agustín Lara's romantic tunes had never had a more willing victim. After dinner by candlelight we had more champagne and held hands over the table. She seemed to have been afflicted with the same virus as I. When we kissed in the taxi on the way home, I realized I had never known what true desire was because I had never been in love before.

Arriving at her home, we discovered she had been locked out by the family she was staying with. She thought it wiser to give some explanation in the morning rather than try to wake them up now; she thought maybe she'd better stay at a hotel. I thought maybe she'd better too, and hurried her off to the nearest one before she could think of the name of some friend or relative to call. In the expensive Hotel Reforma I registered her in a suite and accompanied her to the room. I was weaving a bit by this time from having impressed her with so much champagne, but I told the bellboy to bring another bottle. Linda said she would let me stay "for just one quick drink."

I plied her with several glasses of champagne, but before I could determine their exact effect upon her, I had an overwhelming desire to close my eyes for just a short second.

When I came to it was morning, the sun was streaming in, and Linda was dressing. She came over and laughed at me holding my head and kissed me. She looked so beautiful in just a slip, with her hair swirling around her shoulders. I tried to make up for my lack of amorousness the night before but she said she had to hurry to catch a bus for Taxco.

For an instant I was depressed, but then had a fine idea. I told her I'd borrow a car and drive her, and she said that would be wonderful. A bullfight had to be canceled, but what did that matter? What did anything matter except Linda? So we drove to Taxco, that fairytale town up in the mountains hours away from Mexico City and weeks away from any problems. We stayed at a fine little inn and for three nights and two days we did nothing but enjoy the town and each other. We strolled hand in hand around the cobbled streets and went to the quaint pink cathedral and bought silver trinkets and stared at the American tourists and swam and lay in the sun. I had never known such happiness. But soon my money ran out and Linda had to get back to see a man who had promised her a screen test, so we had to leave Taxco.

I was in the clouds. After we got back to Mexico City I tried to call her but couldn't reach her for several days.

Then when I did see her it was by accident at a party —
and I was taken aback to see she was there with the matador
Fulano de Tal. She was "terribly glad" to see me, however,
and said that she'd been "terribly busy" regarding her
career. We saw each other the next night and once more
it was wonderful. But again it was several days before I
could see her. We had a weekend in Cuernavaca, and it was
almost as good as Taxco. But again she was too involved
to see me for a whole week afterwards. This went on for
months; soon we were in a pattern of the stormiest sort.
Wild wonderful weekends in Acapulco and Guadalajara,
and then she would go out with other men, usually movie
actors, directors, or top matadors, and there would be bitter
accusations and fights and terrible periods when we didn't
see each other and my insides would be eaten out. She had
soon found out, of course, that I was all bluff, neither a
rich nor a successful torero, and though I know she was fond
of me, she craved the best. She was going up rapidly, getting better breaks in the acting world as her charm and
beauty became known to more and more important people.

"It's my job to be seen," she would exclaim. "I love you
darling, but I've got to get somewhere in this life." Her
drive was as consuming as mine had been, with the difference that now I would have chucked my career in a moment
for her, so bewitched by her was I.

Then she stopped seeing me altogether. I suppose she
figured that I was getting nowhere and that an alliance
with me was hurting her with her more important contacts.
I was out of my mind — truly out of my mind — with
jealousy and frustration. I had to see her — but how could
I get her to come to me? Then I hit upon the most
juvenile of plans: I would get myself gored — not seriously,
but just enough to get her sympathy and rekindle the spark.

She would not refuse to see me if I were in a hospital wounded.

I was scheduled to fight in the big Covadonga Festival fight in the plaza in Mexico City. When my bull came out, a large one from San Mateo, I made a few passes with it — and great passes they were, because I didn't care whether I got hit or not. Then I ran out in front of the bull in such a way that I was in a position where the right horn should just graze my hip. However, I miscalculated. The bull, charging at full speed somehow crashed straight into me, the horns on either side of my body. Never have I felt anything so painful as when that animal's head smacked into my stomach and I was slammed into the air. They carried me moaning into the infirmary. The doctor examined me and said, "He's all right — get him out of here."

"Doctor, I'm dying," I groaned. "Take me to the hospital!"

He snorted and sent me back into the arena with my stomach screaming in protest. I hung around the phone all night with a violent ache in my guts, but no call of sympathy came. What a fool love can make of a man!

Finally, the next day when no call had come, I said to myself: Look, you're getting sick from just sitting around mooning about this girl. Do something! I sent word to her that I was leaving immediately for Europe, to fight there. I expected some reaction, but nothing. Then it occurred to me, Why not really go? Then she'd be sorry. I counted up all my money, found I had enough to do it, and made immediate reservations. As I was returning from the steamship line I passed a car agency. There in the window I saw the most beautiful flaming Lincoln Continental. This would really impress her. For a full two minutes I argued with myself about how stupid it would be to buy it, then went in and bought it and felt the guilty glow that only rank self-indulgence can bring.

I must have driven around her house for two hours before she came out, dressed beautifully and hurrying to an appointment.

"Carlos dear, what are you doing here?"

"Just happened to be driving by."

"But this car — whose is it?"

"Oh this thing? I picked it up for Europe. I leave tomorrow."

I kept hoping she'd ask me not to go.

"You must have some good contracts."

If she had said one word, I would have canceled my ticket immediately.

"Dozens," I answered.

"I'm so very glad for you, darling," she said, and I thought I saw tears in her eyes. "Good luck."

She kissed me on the cheek. I started to blurt out all sorts of things, but then a Rolls-Royce, driven by a chauffeur and with a man in the back, pulled up to the curb. She blew me a kiss, got into the car, and drove off.

A week later I arrived in Portugal with my fine rolling asset, almost no money in my pocket, no return passage, and a great ache in my soul. My basic attitude was the infantile one of "By God, I'll become the richest and most famous matador in the world, and then she'll be sorry!" But to show you how completely demoralized and self-deluded I was at this point — I very carefully had brought no fighting equipment. If I had no capes, I couldn't fight and hence I wouldn't have to prove that I wasn't the world's greatest bullfighter and could keep on assuring myself that I was. To further show how completely unrealistic I was, there wasn't a prayer of my being asked to fight in Lisbon after my disastrous season there last time. And Spain was completely out, as the boycott against Mexican toreros was still on.

Once in Portugal, I went completely crazy. I began living the grand life drinking with both hands, and roaring around the cobbled hills of the city in my flashy car. My car caused a sensation, since because of the world war there weren't many modern automobiles in Portugal, and most of the vehicles were twenty years old. The men looked at it enviously and the girls squealed with delight when I offered them a ride. My ego was at such a low ebb that I didn't care how I got admiration, even if it were just by owning a hunk of metal. To forget the face that was always in my mind, I plunged myself into a sea of flesh, and every night I would go out with a different girl, or girls, and make the rounds of the bistros till dawn. These girls were generally actresses, but of the type whose films get confiscated.

All this aimless tearing around caused me to get talked about, at least. I was living like the most successful of toreros, which is probably why one day the impresario called to say that "he might be able to fit me in some place." I answered, "No interest," that I'd come to Europe for fun. I kept on my wild roller-coaster ride, sinking lower and lower as I went faster and faster. A few days later I ran into the impresario again. He asked if I'd changed my mind. "Never fight again," I said. "Just fun." I didn't tell him I'd lost faith — in myself and just about everything else.

My refusals seemed to make me much more desirable. One day at a party when I was full of wine I decided to get rid of him for good. "Look," I said with the arrogance that only a couple of bottles of port can give, "if you're so bloody anxious to get me I'll do it, but on two conditions: 50,000 escudos and only on the same program with Manolete."

I offered him these conditions knowing they were laughably impossible, since 50,000 escudos was a fortune and to insist upon appearing with the greatest star of modern times was deserving of his telling me exactly what he did tell me. "You're crazy!"

But anyway he left me in peace, and I kept throwing my I O U's around like a drunken admiral. Finally I had to sell my beloved car. That very day I bumped into the impresario at a dinner. "Look," he said, "I don't know who's more crazy, you or me. I think it's me. I'm going to accept your offer."

Qué barbaridad! Something had happened that never could. He accepted my terms! After the flops that I had had the past season it was incredible that this could have happened. I was sure that the Lincoln or the brandy after dinner was what really got me the contract, since my artistic merits in the bullring were worthless at this point.

I was suddenly scared.

The fear of cold reality shook me so that I immediately cut out the drinking and the women and the night life and started to try to get myself in some kind of shape. I had only ten days in which to do it. I also had to order uniforms, sashes, ties, capes, everything from Spain, since I had brought nothing. Hurriedly I got out on the ranch of a friend who let me fight calves in his private ring, and I managed to cram in a lot of training every day. The frightening hour was rushing at me when I would appear side by side with the "Monster of the Bullring," Manuel Rodríguez, the most important day of my career.

How impressed Linda would be that I had not only met her idol Manolete, but was actually competing with him!

7

WITH MANOLETE! Me — me with Manolete! I still couldn't quite understand how this had ever come about. But now it was all set and in front of me I saw a big poster that roared "Manolete, Morenito de Talavera, and Carlos Arruza"! The Portuguese bullfighting fans could talk of little else but Manolete, and they were delighted that a figure of such magnitude was fighting in their bullring.

My first desire was to meet him the moment he arrived in Lisbon. Dressing myself up to look as much like a real bullfighter as possible, I went to the hotel where he was staying.

"Is — is Manolete — could I meet him?" I asked the concierge.

"He can see no one," the man answered coldly.

A lot of people were milling around from the bullfighting world, but I didn't dare ask them about him. I went to the bar and had a drink (of soda water now) to see if he might not come down, and then I could snatch an opportunity to introduce myself. But he didn't show up. I left after a while but returned later in the afternoon, and still I couldn't get to see him. I knew him only from the photos and, like any aficionado, I knew what everyone knew, that he was ugly, that he was a phenomenon with a bull, that his was a new concept of bullfighting, and that he fought brilliantly with almost all the animals that he drew, no matter what their styles or conditions.

Throughout my career I have gone to the drawing of the bulls very few times, and almost never since I took the alternative. That day I went, just to see if Manolete might not go the drawing and then I could get to meet him before the action started. But I was disappointed again, because they told me that he never went to see the bulls before they came out of the toril. At least the greatest bullfighter in the world and I had that much in common, and foolishly, I clung to that insignificant fact.

I wanted to go see him at the hotel after the drawing and introduce myself with some pretext or other, or simply to wish him luck, but I didn't dare. Instead, I went home to prepare myself for one of the most important happenings of my life.

That afternoon the plaza de toros was a terrifying monster, since it was jammed to the eaves with people who had paid large amounts to see the world's greatest torero fight two bulls; they would have filled the stands just to see him walk across the ring in the parade, so great was his attraction. As has always been my custom I was the first matador to arrive at the cuadrilla gate. Very nervous I was too. ("Nervous," I should tell you, is a highly technical taurine term meaning "scared to death.") A little while later Morenito de Talavera arrived and I was introduced to him. A pretty big star in Spain, he seemed a modest person and we chatted pleasantly for a while as we had a last smoke. Soon we heard a murmur, the murmur that one hears only on important occasions. Manolete was coming! The crowds gave way before him as though for a king.

Manuel Rodríguez, "Manolete"

I was struck immediately by his face. He wasn't ugly the way the photos made him appear. It was a good face, though scarred and sad. He was only twenty-seven, but he looked forty. Terribly serious, almost tragic-looking, he barely managed the hint of a smile in answer to the reverent greetings that the people gave him as he made his way through the crowd. I noticed that no one patted him on the back, the way they do with other toreros, any more than one would pat a bishop on the back as he made his way up the aisle to the altar. The moment I saw him I understood that this man had been born to be nothing more or less than a bullfighter. I saw that in just his regal mien and the way he carried himself and the way his uniform sat on his body. I believe he even smelled like a bull-fighter.

I longed to be introduced to him, to shake his hand, to get to know him. But he moved away from where I was to the other side of the gate without so much as a glance at me. Then a friend said, "Like to meet him?"

"Would I!" I answered.

I eagerly followed him over to Manolete.

"Maestro," my friend said, "this is Arruza, the new Mexican matador."

Manolete turned his haughty face, and looked vacantly at me with those heavy-lidded eyes. All that the man muttered was "Qué tal — how goes it?" so dryly, so stiffly, so aloofly that he sent a chill through me. Then he turned away.

I gave him some kind of stammering answer, somehow, and then I withdrew. Or rather I slunk away. Afterwards they took a photograph of us together, neither of us saying a word to the other.

More than ever I wanted to have luck. I really yearned for it that afternoon. He hadn't even known I was there!

He would have treated even a banderillo with more respect, I thought. I'm a matador after all, not the greatest by any means, but still I'm a full matador! I felt a flush of embarrassment when I thought of all the goings and comings I had done just to get to meet him, and then he treated me like this.

The trumpet blew and the corrida began.

I am not going to give a pass-by-pass description of it. I'll simply try to convey the impression that the bullfighting of Manolete made on me that first time I saw him.

It was something totally new to me. I had never seen anybody place himself so close to a bull and then wait out with such calm and surety the charges — vicious and treacherous ones mostly — of his first enemy.

With the cape I saw a frightening tranquility, and I marveled at his half-verónica. That half-verónica of Manolete! He'd stand straight as a ramrod, the left arm stiff at his hip, the right swinging with the smoothness and slowness of a pendulum, and with that majestic economy of his, his cape would describe a sort of fan over the sand, while the beast brushed against his belt, its spikes grazing the silk and gold of his costume. Then when he grabbed the muleta and went out with the bull, I really saw and understood the true greatness of this torero. I remember that after the dedication he placed himself at some distance from his first bull, the worst of the afternoon, with his body composed and serene. He cited for an unmoving, statuesque Pass of Death. It never would have occurred to me to begin a faena with a bull like that in such a manner, without at least having doubled the animal with half a dozen punishing passes so that later I could remain quiet on a few fancy passes. That's the way Maestro Solís had taught us, and that's the way all the matadors did it. But Manolete had a completely different idea. Right from the beginning he

Absolutely still!

planted his feet on the sand and remained there, still—absolutely still!

"Ah huh, toro!" he commanded the bull in his deep, sad Cordoban accent. The bull pawed the sand and prepared to charge.

In that moment I turned to a friend who was watching the performance from the passageway, and stated confidently, "I'll cut my head off if this uncle stays there!"

If I had been a man of my word, I'd be wandering around now decapitated. For these words were no sooner out of my mouth than I saw the impossible in bullfighting. It happened not once, but five, six, seven, I don't know how many times that bull passed by his sash without his moving back one millimeter, with a style and show of courage that made

me gasp. He did things with that bull which were incredible, incredible for the distance in which he cited the animal and forced it to charge. His greatness stemmed from the fact that he was the only fighter who dominated the bull while at the same time remaining absolutely still and calm. He dominated it by simply waiting out the charges in an incredible manner. Since Manolete, the doubling, punishing passes have almost disappeared from bullfighting. They aren't needed any more, because this señor showed us that a bull can be dominated simply by a

person's having the courage — more courage than the bull — to withstand its charges without jumping back out of the way.

On his second enemy, which was a very honest and good bull, he brought the house down. I saw bullfighting with the left hand, the *natural,* after having cited from a distance at which I had never imagined a bullfighter could place himself, with a marvelous slow, suave, and controlling style. This was completely new to me. I was almost glad that there had existed a boycott which had prohibited us Mexicans from fighting in Spain, since it seemed impossible that anyone could compete alongside this man.

I was lucky enough to have a fairly successful afternoon, in my way, and, thank goodness, I had brains enough not to try to compete with Manolete at his own classic game. I managed to win what applause I got by doing every kind of wild thing I could think of and every trick of the bull-ring that I'd ever learned from Maestro Solís or anyone else. When one sees that one can't better the performance of a competitor, the best thing to do is to try to do the opposite of what he has done. Therefore, if Manolete did

It seemed impossible that anyone could compete alongside this man.

Whirling molinetes.

perfect classic verónicas, I would do flashy kneeling passes with the cape; if he did naturals, I would do the whirling molinetes.

That is how I first knew the man who for me was the greatest bullfighter of this age. I didn't really know him then, of course, since I misinterpreted his manner, mistaking the reticence and seriousness with which he took bullfighting for dislike of me. I just didn't understand him; when dressed in uniform, and in or around a bullring, Manolete changed.

Once when a reporter asked him "Why is it you never smile in the plaza?" he answered, "Esto de los toros es una cosa muy seria" — This business of the bulls is a very serious thing.

8

After my presentation in Lisbon with Manolete, I realized that without doubt all of us bullfighters were entering into a great evolution in the art of bullfighting. Now I couldn't think of anything else but how I was going to adapt myself to this new school. As I saw it, this was the only way that I could become a real figure in the fiesta brava. Simultaneously there hammered in my brain the idea that I would have to invade the same terrains as Manolete, but I must not fall into an imitation of him, which would be as disastrous as not adapting myself to this new style at all.

That afternoon in Lisbon, I didn't miss a single movement of his. It was indelibly imprinted in my mind, detail for detail, movement by movement, gesture by gesture. So great was the impression that now, after all these years, I can see it just as though it were a motion picture in front of my eyes. The first thing I saw in Manolete was that he invaded an impossible terrain, "crossing" with the bull in a straight line and, incredibly enough, on two or three occasions, even going so far as to go past the near horn which he was citing. Maestro Solís had warned that this was fatal, and yet Manolete had got away with it! I lay awake all night thinking about it.

What would happen if I went out there and had enough guts to reach the same distance and, once there, if I crossed all the way over to the opposite horn? Maestro Solís could slap his forehead and say "Impossible!" Yet what Manolete had done that afternoon was impossible too. If I could pull this off, I was sure that it would result in something new, without falling into an imitation.

Every night that next week I spent tossing and turning, because this coming Sunday I was fighting again, this time with Domingo Ortega. I spent most of each day running and rerunning the movies of Manolete, and practicing, with an imaginary bull, what I was going to try to do. Every night I fought and refought the corrida.

It was the custom to start to circle bulls that were slow to charge by citing them as one crossed with them, but at a distance that was more or less sensible and without even taking a step closer toward the bull. Now we were going to see if my theory that each step be *toward* the bull as well as in a circle would work out!

As the day approached, I got an attack of nerves and began to hope two bulls would come out that would *not* give me an opportunity of experimenting on my plan, but would rather be easier ones of honest, long charges so that I could show off my repertoire better. But at the same time I was very curious to know if my scheme could make me look good on a sedentary, slow-charging, difficult bull. If I could accomplish that, I would have managed to do two very important things: first, I would be able to get a fight from nine out of ten bulls that are sent to the bullrings, and second, I would be a success without being a copy of Manolete — and this was very important, because seconds are never any good.

Normal citing   The Manolete point   The Arruza point   The charge

Arruza's amazing new style of "crossing."

From this standpoint, then, the bullfight that was closing in on me was of enormous importance. If I had guts enough to invade those terrains up to "the Manolete point" in the first place and then afterwards to "cross with" the bull, I could rest easy. This would mark without doubt an evolution in bullfighting, and it would also help me discover my own personal style, which I had never yet really found.

Finally, after terrible doubts and waitings and sleepless nights, the Sunday on which I was to perform "hand to hand" with Domingo Ortega arrived. My first bull was a pretty good one and didn't give me the opportunity to try out my theory. It charged fiercely and hard and from a long distance away.

My second one was the opposite. If I had drawn a bull like this before having seen Manolete, I would have simply

lined the bull up with a few uninspired passes and then dispatched it. But things were different now. Nervously, I took the muleta and went out toward that animal which was just waiting for me solidly, wickedly, as though saying, "I won't charge you unless you come in, way in, unless you goad me into it by showing me you're willing to commit suicide."

I managed to screw up my courage, and with the muleta in my right hand, I started shuffling my feet toward him. Closer and closer I came. It looked first at my hip, then at the muleta, then back at my hip. "Toro!" I shouted as I kept edging forward and across the line of its charge.

I could feel the cold sweat on my face and my shirt clammy on my back as I saw the bull staring at my hip, trying to make up its mind which target to go for. I heard the audience hush as they saw me preparing to do something very strange. Now I was in line with the near horn, the way Manolete had been. My first impulse was to quit there. But I swallowed and made my feet keep shuffling closer. And closer. *And closer.*

I heard the small noises of the crowd in back of me. "What the devil's he trying to do?"

I was beyond the point of no return now, for if I tried to withdraw he would surely charge into me. I have learned that when you reach a certain point with a bull you cannot vacillate, you cannot give down an inch, or he will be on you. They sense your indecision. You must make him think that you have more guts than he has. No faltering, no uncertainty, you must keep moving forward or you are lost. I had to keep going, had to keep crossing with him, and *will* him into hooking the muleta and not my hip. I was right on top of him now, not two feet away. It seemed impossible to me that he could miss me, even if he tried to.

Suddenly he charged. His entire length brushed against

His entire length brushed against me.

me and the barrel of his rib cage bumped me back, but the horn had missed me!

It worked!

A great gasp went up from the audience when they realized what they had seen. And then when I repeated it again and again, the gasps turned into roars, incredulous roars.

That afternoon I was carried out on the shoulders of the crowd. And this, with a bull I should otherwise have discarded as unfightable as quickly as possible. In all the seasons I had performed there — and this was my fourth — I had never seen a torero leave on the shoulders of the crowd, in spite of the fact I'd seen some fine performances by many matadors. What better proof for my new system?

I knew in my heart that no one, not even the fabulous Manolete, had ever worked closer to the horns, and the newspapers the next day bore this out: "Young Arruza did some rare and astonishing things yesterday."

I suddenly had a great many offers to fight in Portugal, which I couldn't accept, since I had to leave for Spain to meet my mother, who was arriving on the boat at La Coruña in a few days. I would be very grateful later for not having taken those contracts.

Happily I set off for Spain, thinking of the wonderment that I was going to cause in Mexico if I could just develop my new form of bullfighting a little more. Especially in Mexico would it go over, I thought, since the Mexican bulls are always more reluctant to charge than the ones in Spain and Portugal. I was so happy with my new style that it seemed impossible that they wouldn't give me some contracts in Mexico now for the big season. There could be certain difficulties, of course, because of my performances of the past year, but I'd show them how I had improved. I couldn't fight in Spain, because of the political boycott of Mexican bullfighters, and this disappointed me terribly. In Madrid I got myself a fine manager named Andrés Gago, but of course there was nothing for him to manage as long as the boycott continued.

Then one day it happened. I was walking down the Gran Vía one morning when I bumped into a bullfighter who said to me, "I'll be there on the eighteenth of July — and you better be good too!"

At first I thought he was joking, and pretty unfunnily at that. But he soon convinced me. It was true. I was to be a sort of guinea pig to see how the people of Spain reacted to a Mexican's fighting in Spain. If everything went well, the boycott would be off indefinitely.

I immediately ordered myself a new uniform and then sat

around waiting, waiting for what Manolo and I had dreamed of back in bullfighting school.

My presentation in Madrid!

Then four days before I was to appear in that arena, Manolete put up a performance that made me want to hide my head with the shame of my own inadequate powers and run from bullfighting forever. Manolete immortalized two bulls and glorified bullfighting as it never had been done before. My friend the Peruvian matador Montani and I were high up in inexpensive seats in the arena, but we didn't miss a single detail of that performance as Manolete took on two large bulls and fought them so closely that his entire uniform was bloody from having brushed against the animal's shoulders so many times. Never had I seen such purity of style, such bravery, such grace, such command!

Can you imagine my state of mind? What could I do so soon afterwards?

My first thought was, Maybe I'd better see my manager and the impresario, tell them sorry, but I was just not going to fight on the eighteenth of July. Please excuse little Carlos today, he has a cold. Then as we were coming back on the bus from the plaza de toros, I heard two aficionados who, like all the other passengers, were talking about the tremendous success of Manolete. One of them said, "Hey, what about this 'Ruso' [Russian] who's announced for this next fight? What's he going to do after this, eh?"

They didn't even know my name correctly.

"Nothing, chico," answered the other. "Just slink back to Moscow."

These two aficionados made up my mind definitely, only this "Ruso" wasn't going back to Moscow, but back to Mexico.

"Just get another boy," I said to the impresario.

"Here we practically have the boycott fixed and you pull

this," he said. "You'll ruin everything. You owe it to the other toreros!"

"But I'm not ready for Madrid," I said. "I'm not ready to follow a Manolete triumph. And if I flop now they won't let me back in this area even to sell peanuts!"

"It's now or never."

Between him and Gago they convinced me that this was the terrible truth: now or never. All right, I said finally and wretchedly, make it now.

Just before the fight my mother arrived, and her presence helped me. It's strange, even though she hated the idea of my bullfighting she now accepted the fact that I was a matador and took it for granted that I was unquestionably the world's best, and would be recognized as such shortly. A highly determined woman, she had immense confidence in me and in the fact that I could do anything that she set my mind to. Now she set her mind to setting my mind at ease about the forthcoming nightmare, and after two days of her cheery, iron presence I was almost anxious to get out there in front of the thing I dreaded most in the world: the public of Madrid.

The night before the fight she thought it would take my mind off things to go to a Mexican movie. Five minutes after we were in the theater Linda's face was flashed on the screen; she had the second lead in the film. I was pleased to see she was on her way, but it was upsetting to see her. It revived too many pleasant and unpleasant memories, so I suggested that we leave. I don't know whether it was Linda or my underlying desire to not fight the next day — as we went down the steep balcony stairs in the dark I tripped and fell two flights, while the audience cried out in alarm. I got up, bruised and ashamed of my clumsiness, but without anything broken, for which I was sorry, since I was still in good enough condition to fight. If I couldn't even handle theater stairs, what about bulls? The next morning, after a completely sleepless night, I woke up my mother and we went to Mass, where I asked my real manager for Her protection and guidance. When I got back to the hotel the battle of nerves began as people began telling me rumors that would have caused the most tranquil person in the world to blow up.

"I understand that the other toreros who are unhappy about the boycott arrangements are going to throw themselves into the ring on your first bull," one said.

Another volunteered: "Somebody said a bunch are going to lay for you and beat you up on the way to the ring."

Common sense and Gago and my mother convinced me these were just rumors, but nevertheless it had me in a bad state of nerves. At two o'clock I said to Vargas, the sword boy, "Well, get the uniform ready."

The battle of nerves began.

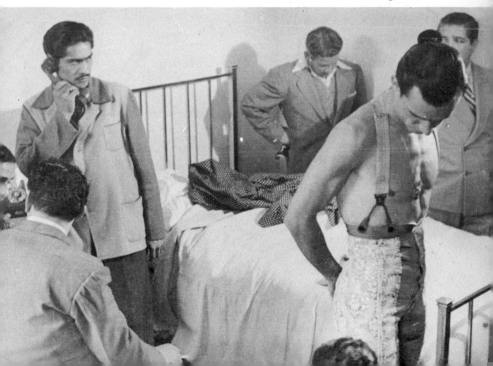

"What uniform?" he answered.

"Didn't he send it?" Andrés exclaimed.

"Who?"

"The tailor! The man who was supposed to make it!"

Vargas telephoned. "Where's the suit?"

"Working on it," replied the tailor cheerily.

"Working on it," Vargas relayed.

"Working on it!" I exclaimed. "Good God!"

Then came pacing, glancing at the watches every five minutes, calling every ten minutes to find out how the uniform was coming, my mother feeding me nerve pills and soothing talk. Finally when it didn't show up and the time was running out I said, "Look, there must be some other bullfighters here in the hotel. We can borrow a suit from one of them."

Gago chewed slowly on his cigar. "Yes, there's one. It's —"

"Go ask him for a uniform!"

Gago hesitated.

"It's Manolete."

I swallowed. "Manolete?"

"Yes."

"The only one in the whole hotel?"

"Yes."

"Well, just go ask the bastard if we can't borrow one of his uniforms!"

He went down, talked to him, and in two minutes Manolete's sword boy appeared and handed Vargas a resplendent gold and blue suit of lights as aloofly and condescendingly as his matador might have done. I hurriedly struggled into it, and it was a struggle, since the skintight costumes are designed for only one owner and this wrinkled and bulged in the wrong places. However, I now had a suit even if I would look like a clown. Just as I was about to go out the door the little tailor puffed cheerily into the room carrying my suit of lights. With a bellow of shattered nerves, I stripped off Manolete's suit and put on my own. My mother gave me her blessing and then it was time.

A voice, smug and secure, announced, "Well, off to the battleground," and away we went, with me in a dazed condition. In the car, as we went through the crowded streets, I really began to worry about the bulls. They were from a ranch called Vicente Muriel, which I'd never heard of before. And on these unknown quantities hung all my dreams of glory in Spain. My God, wouldn't night hurry up and come so that we would know how all this would end! But in order for the long awaited night to arrive the terribly feared afternoon would first have to pass.

We arrived at the ring, and when I got out of the car I glanced around me apprehensively, a little worried about the rumor that they were going to try to beat me up. But instead of blows I received slaps on the back and good wishes. "Luck, boy, take heart!" And as I walked to the back of the ring there was one comment made by a funny little toothless beggar which almost made me laugh and did a lot for me: "If you can fight like a bullfighter the way you look like a bullfighter, today I'm going to have me a good time and get crosseyed drunk afterwards and beat up my wife!"

As I came up to the gate of the cuadrillas there were photographs, greetings, embraces. It was all too much for my nerves. And meanwhile the plaza was filling up to the top. Finally came the trumpet, the trumpet of glory, of failure, or of death. We made the parade in the center of a funereal silence which struck me as very strange, because I was accustomed to the beautiful shout of the Mexican audiences when the trumpet blew to begin the bullfight. We received handclaps, a smattering of applause as we strode across the ring, and that was all. I looked up at that knowing, cold, venerable crowd and shuddered.

Then the trumpet sounded for my first bull. In a moment

the bull pounded out of the toril, silvery gray, with tremendous horns jutting from its head and with a dangerous style of attacking that I spotted from the first testing cape pass that my banderillero gave it. For the first time in my life, since my initial childhood encounter, I truly regretted being a bullfighter. There flooded into my body at that moment a frightening panic, not so much fear of the beast but rather fear of being rejected by the crowd, which Blasco Ibáñez calls "the only true beast in the plaza." It was all too much for me.

I was bad, very bad with the cape. My verónicas were suspiciously like those which had appalled Maestro Solís that first day. The bull hooked radically toward the fence and with each cape pass he backed me up and closed me in more and more, until finally I was forced to throw down my cape and get out by piling over the barrera as best I could. I could feel the embarrassed boredom and restlessness of the crowd. How did this young Mexican ever get this fight in the first place?

The trumpet sounded for the banderillas. My instinct told me that this animal, while terrible for the cape, would be good for the sticks. As far as the "palitroques" went, my instinct had seldom failed me, so as my banderillero picked up the brightly papered sticks and started away from the barrera I said, "Wait!"

I snatched them out of his hands and loped out toward the bull. Fifty feet from him I stopped. He looked at me curiously and I looked back at him. Then I slowly started stalking him, casually, heel and toeing my way toward him. Whereas he had dominated me with the cape, I would show him who was master on this maneuver. I approached him so cockily and calmly — forty feet, thirty feet, twenty feet — that he didn't charge and just stared at me as though mesmerized. Holding the banderillas down at my side I kept

I would show him
who was master.

coming at him, now dangerously close. Fifteen feet, fourteen feet —

This was to be *poder a poder* style. Usually the matador
breaks off to the side long before this, so as to take advantage
of cutting in on the bull at an angle. But I was practically
on top of the animal now. I heard the crowd hushed and

The famous Arruza pair of banderillas in Madrid, 1944.

The famous pair by Gaona in Pamplona, 1915.

expectant. I realized I could come no closer, and as I broke off to the side as fast as I could go the animal lunged forward with a bellow. As we came together, instead of bending over the safe way, I raised my arms as high as possible, kept my body absolutely straight and let the animal come into me so close that for a fraction of a second I actually felt his horn graze the sash across my stomach. As we were one there in the center of the ring I flashed down with the banderillas and barbed them into his withers, pushed on them to help me pivot away out of the crescent of the horns, and then I spun to the side as the bull's momentum made it hurtle by me, bucking and distracted by the sting of the fishhook points. I knew it was the greatest pair of banderillas I had ever placed in my life even before I heard the roar of the astonished crowd. They were amazed. They never thought anyone that bad with the cape could be that good with the sticks.* I placed the next two pairs of banderillas almost as well, and the crowd cheered and rubbed its hands in anticipation for the last third of the fight.

But this bull just wasn't right for me for either the cape or muleta, and it was bad in the wrong way — not bad in the good way, the *tardo,* slow-to-charge way, where I could try out my Lisbon experiment again, but bad in a distracted, bronco, hooking way that made it impossible for me to shine. I was even worse with the muleta than with the cape. It was terrible to lose the audience after I had them captured with the sticks, but absolutely nothing I tried with this animal came out right. Fortunately I managed to kill quickly, but when I came back to the fence and Gago handed me a towel to wipe my sweaty face, I could hear the mutterings of the crowd. They felt defrauded. They didn't even boo me — I wasn't worth it.

---

* The next day the papers compared this pair of banderillas to the pair by Gaona in Pamplona in 1915, considered the greatest ever placed.

"A good banderillero for Manolete, and that's all," I heard one man say.

I was so ashamed I couldn't raise my face. My flop couldn't have been more complete and definite. During the performances of the second and third bull by the other bullfighters I decided that I was either going to triumph on my next enemy or right there in the ring I would remain for the rest of my life. I thought of my mother, kneeling at home in the hotel praying for me. I thought of my friends in Mexico, Linda, my dead brother and father. I would not leave the bullring that afternoon on foot, with a failure behind me. On occasions, life furnishes us with a transcendental moment, and this was mine.

My second bull came out, black, fat, and beautiful, with a pair of long sharp horns. The banderilleros ran him back and forth for me, I saw that he hooked honestly, and I went out toward him, determined to triumph or to die.

I don't know how, I am unable to explain what I did or how I did it. I just tried to do everything I had ever learned, from Maestro Solís, from my brother, and Manolete, and do it all as gracefully and as close to those horns as humanly possible. But I don't know the details. All I know is that by the time the act of the banderillas came around the plaza was already white with handkerchiefs as the sign that they wanted me to be granted an ear! And then later I know that somehow I suddenly found myself taking laps around the ring, lap after lap, with both ears of the bull in my hands, the top award that is given in Madrid. I know that I heard, as though I were dreaming, deafening ovations, similar to those which I had imagined many years before when I had first seen the outside of this ring. But I don't know exactly what I did to achieve all this. I had triumphed, I knew that much, because I had the ears in my hands, and I heard the ovations and the cries of the crowd. In order to learn what

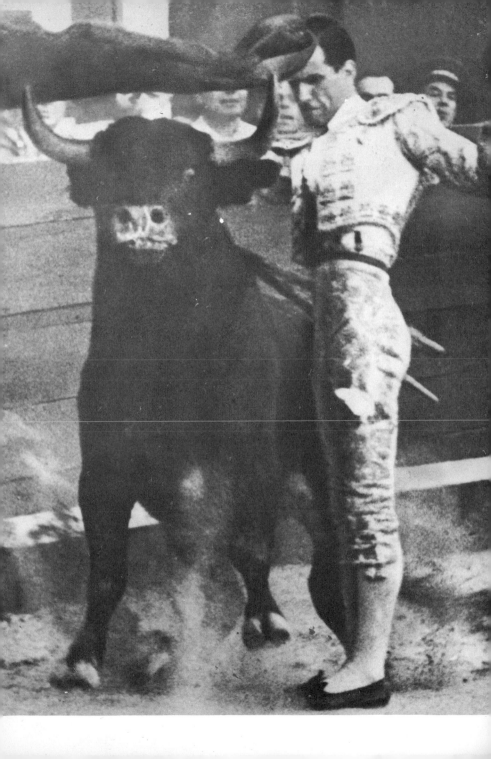

I had done I had to ask the ecstatic Gago and afterwards, the following day, to read the reviews in the newspapers.

"A completely new style . . ." the *Daily ABC* critic said. "One has to see it to believe that all the accepted theories of bullfighting could be so easily broken . . ." Said another, "I still don't believe those banderillas." Said still another: "The perfect torero, is this young cyclone from Mexico!"

I had triumphed, yes I had really triumphed!

I still believe that it wasn't I who triumphed, since I don't even remember or know what I did. I believe that inside of me there appeared the spirit of my father and my brother and that their hands swung the cape, and I believe that my holy Manager sent them to me to do it.

I came to and returned to being just me, myself, once I had the ears of the bull in my hands.

9

THAT TRIUMPH in Madrid carried me instantly to the foreground of the bullfighting scene. The public had been searching eagerly for an opponent to Manolete, and this corrida was the first step toward occupying such an enviable position. Of course neither the public nor I had any illusions, since one good afternoon in the life of a bullfighter means nothing except the fact that it makes one have to be good on the fight that follows and then one must keep on doing it, so that the crowds realize that it hasn't been just a matter of chance nor the inspiration of a moment.

But at least the first step had been taken, and taken with determination, thanks to the miracle of my second bull in Madrid. After the fight that night we went to eat dinner at the restaurant of the Recoletos jai alai, where my entrance created a stir. "Don't look now but . . ."

Of course, this pleases any neophyte performer when he realizes that he is being recognized by a crowd outside the ring, too, and in my case the satisfaction was greater, since twenty-four hours before I was a complete unknown — "El Ruso," as those two aficionados on the bus had called me.

Now I had a week in front of me before my presentation in Barcelona. It would be the 25th of July. For this fight there was a set of bulls from a ranch with a poor reputation, and Gago didn't like the idea. Certainly not now after my triumph in Madrid, since all the aficionados were waiting to see what I was going to do, to see if it hadn't been all just luck. Therefore, as soon as we arrived in Barcelona, he went out to the corrals behind the big plaza de toros. Gago is little and gentle-mannered, but no one knows more than he how to handle things, and no one can be tougher in a gentle way.

"Those are bulls?" he snorted when the impresario showed him the scrubby, crooked-horned creatures intended for my fight. Then he glanced into the next corral and saw six hand-picked, uniform, sleek beauties from the famous Cobaleda ranch. "Now those are something more like it." Gago was himself a matador, from the age of fifteen until he retired at thirty-five, and he really knew his bulls.

"Ah, but those are for the great Manolete in two weeks."

"Unless we get those bulls, Carlos doesn't fight here Sunday!"

"But I've sold every seat in the ring!" the man protested.

"You can refund their money, because without those bulls we don't fight."

"But if I give you those bulls, then Manolete will be furious and he might never fight here."

"Look," said Gago in his irrestible, confidential tone. "Within one week — one week mind you — Carlos will be as big a drawing card as Manolete, and I'll tell you what we'll do; no matter how big we get, we'll come fight in your ring anytime you ask."

Only Gago's great gift of gab — what the Andaluzes call *labia* — could have sold the poor man this bill of goods. Manolete refused to fight again in Barcelona for the entire season because of it, but we got the bulls.

I stayed at a second-rate hotel, but one which Gago said would be very good luck for me, and he was rarely wrong. I was unknown to the Barcelona crowd and they went to the plaza that day not expecting too much because there was a rumor that I was just a good banderillero and that's all. Strangely enough, when it came time for the banderillas on my first bull I was a terrible letdown. Just the opposite from my first bull in Madrid, this bull was bad for the banderillas, but oh God, when it came time for the muleta, what a sweet dream of an animal he turned out to be! He was on rails, and I could do anything I felt like with him. When I dropped him with one thrust, I was awarded both ears and the tail, the maximum of trophies. I had to take several laps around the ring also, and when I came up to the fence Gago gave me a big excited slap on the back. "Better than Madrid!" he said. Of course I was deliriously happy, but I answered, "How could you help it with an animal like that" — and it was the truth. But then my second bull came out, and the skeptics in the crowd said knowingly to each other. "Now, my friend, now let's see you try all that fancy filigree stuff on this bug!"

They didn't know it, but my heart leapt when I saw this difficult, reluctant-to-charge, stubborn "bug" of a bull; it was made to order for my "Lisbon style." The crowd booed the bull so loudly because of its reluctance to charge that I was afraid the presidente might order the substitute bull instead. I quickly ran out into the ring and flipped the cape behind my back for a gaonera pass. I offered the bull the right side of the cloth that showed behind my legs and he just looked at it, refusing to charge. Then I began shuffling around him, chanting, "Ah-hah, toro," shaking the cloth. I crossed over beyond the line of the near horn and the crowd gasped. Still the bull did not charge, so I kept shuffling forward until I was standing four feet from him, and right between his horns. Still he didn't charge. Once again I was in a position from which there was no return. If I retreated back the way I'd come I would surely get gored; the bull was about to charge and any motion such as walking away would cause him to crash into my hip. I just needed the guts to go forward. I *had* to go forward, so forward I went. Now I had circled so far that I was citing his off horn, something that had never been seen before in this plaza de toros. I heard moanings from the hushed crowd: "No, boy, no, no!" It looked impossible to them, as though the only way the bull could get by me would be by going behind my legs, not in front of them. Then I saw the shoulder muscles of the bull bunch up as he lunged forward toward my thighs. "Toro!" I shouted and flicked the edge of the cape hard and he veered away from me slightly to hook at the cape. I didn't move my feet back, but I had to go up on my toes and suck in my stomach as much as I could to keep from getting spiked. The round side of the lowered right horn grazed my legs and then the entire length of the black body brushed against my stomach as he hurtled by me.

When the stunned crowd realized I hadn't been hit they set up a deafening clamor, which kept up for the rest of the fight — everything I tried that afternoon turned out right. The animal couldn't have been more perfect for my Lisbon style. When I topped off the muleta work by dropping the animal with a good thrust, the hoarse crowd insisted that I be given both ears, the tail, and — for the first time in Barcelona's history — a hoof!

The people swarmed into the ring, hoisted me on their shoulders and carried me from the plaza de toros all the way into the city back to my hotel, the good-luck hotel. There they made me and my mother come out on the balcony to wave to the big crowd below. It was all quite marvelous,

I didn't move my feet back.

and, if I'd had their addresses I think I would have gone to the home of every single one of them to shake their hands. My room was filled with aficionados, all of them wild with joy. How I remembered a time that I had said to my brother: "Carai, Manolo, what a long way we are from being bull-fighters, since nobody has come to see us after the fight." Now I could include myself among real bullfighters, since this wasn't a room, this was a whole plaza de toros, judging by the number of people in it.

The next day the newspaper clippings were slightly un-believable. There were even poems, songs, and sonnets writ-ten in honor of "El Ciclón," as the newspapers were now re-ferring to me. I never believed that I would be capable of causing such collective madness. And then the following days — the attention, the admiration, and the wonderful way that they treated me wherever I went was amazing. For example, in the afternoons I would go to the movies. I barely had got to the box office to buy tickets when they would say, "Here, you don't pay anything Don Carlos — come in and have a good time!" This occurred in three dif-ferent moviehouses. In restaurants the same thing hap-pened and the shoeshine boys insisted on shining my shoes free. From an unknown to all this was a dream.

"El Ciclón Mejicano" was announced the following Sun-day with Domingo Ortega and El Andaluz, and for the first time in my life I had the thrill of seeing a strip of paper plastered over the bullfight posters saying, "No tickets left!" Interest to see me in other parts of Spain was increasing day after day, upon learning of my successes at Barcelona, and soon there was organized a big event in a city of the province of Murcia called Cieza. There, in an atmosphere of tre-mendous expectation, I saw my name announced next to Manolete's for the first time in a Spanish bullring.

I said to myself: "Now we'll see, Señor Knight of the Sad

Countenance, if I can't make you notice me a little more this time."

This fight was important, very important, not only for me but for my now numerous "arrucistas." The papers gave it a big buildup, because since the Barcelona success everyone was saying that maybe here at last was a rival for the heretofore unrivaled Manolete. People had hoped that Pepe Luis Vázquez, for me one of the greatest of all time, would be the one, but he had fallen by the wayside after a frightening goring near the left eye the year before.° Now I was the big hope, they said, and all the more so because my style was so completely opposite from Manolete's, even though evolved from it.

The poor little town of Cieza was inundated by the people who poured in from all Spain for this event. Most of the people were ardent manoletistas and had come to see this Mexican upstart make a fool of himself. But I had many enthusiastic supporters too who would have given anything to see me "give the bath" to Manolete. I was almost as nervous as before the Madrid fight.

° "It wouldn't be so bad if it were my leg," Pepe Luis says, "but every time I look in the mirror I see my destroyed face and I am afraid."

Pepe Luis Vázquez

Of course he cut both ears off both his bulls.

That afternoon Manolete was granted special permission to fight out of turn because he had to appear the next day at the other end of the country. So he just saw me on my first bull, where I did miserably. Of course he cut both ears off both his bulls, and justly so. My supporters were sunk, and those people who had never seen me before laughed at the crazy idea that this was the man who was supposed to be a threat to Manolete. I was booed on all sides as I went out for my last bull. But again this bull, while it looked terrible to everyone else, was the perfect type for my Lisbon style.

So when the bull was dragged out twenty minutes later, it went without its ears, tail, and, unbelievably, a hoof. The arrucistas were delirious, babbling with joy and vindication, and my enemies were silenced temporarily.

When I arrived jubilantly back at the hotel, Manolete was just leaving, dressed in ordinary clothes, with his ever-present dark glasses and followed by his banderilleros. We stalked by each other coldly, and as he got in the car his manager, Camará, grunted, "Well, how'd it go?"

Gago smiled sweetly. "Hubo patita," he said casually as though this were an everyday occurrence, "there was a hoof."

"A hoof!"

They all seemed to grow hard-faced. Manolete leaned forward as if to exclaim in disbelief, but then he sat back as though it were too much effort. He looked so bored and world-weary, so confident in his position of the Number One.

The perfect type for my "Lisbon style."

They drove off, and as I watched the car go down the road I thought: I'm sorry you missed it today, Your Majesty, but we'll try to repeat for you. Your throne is not as secure as it once was.

The battle was on! The manoletistas began warning us, "We'll see how the next one goes, friend — better cinch your knee tassels up well for that one!"

The real battle was between our managers to get us together again, to come to an agreement with the impresarios on the question of money. Gago would say: "Exactly what he gets we get!" and Camará would retort: "I have the greatest in the world and no one gets the same as he!"

I don't know how they resolved it, since I always left the money matters up to Gago, but they agreed to a "rematch" in Villanueva del Arzobispo. The mere fact that in a few short months I had suddenly been catapulted from an unknown into a position where I could bargain with the great Manolete was an astounding thing. But I was a different person now, and I realized how I had grown artistically when my old friend and banderillero Ricardo Aguilar arrived from Mexico in time for the second Manolete fight. (I had sent for him as soon as I saw how wonderful the outlook appeared for the season.)

This man, who had been with me since I was a young boy and had seen me do everything he thought I was capable of, calmly and with no change of expression now watched me fight with his mouth wide open, and when I turned my back on the bull and walked over to the fence with the crowd roaring, he simply gasped: "Qué bruto — what a brute you've become!" It was the best praise I could be given.

That day I cut ears off both bulls, and strangely enough, Manolete got nothing. My stock soared to the skies all over Spain, which showed the reputation Manolete had; the fact that I had cut ears on a program where Manolete had not, did more for me than having had a great success in Madrid without Manolete on the program.

I was launched now in the biggest way possible and I wasn't going to lose what I had gained for anything in the world. I fought practically every day for the rest of the season, many times with Manolete, and on every one I went out into the plaza as though my entire career rested on the outcome of this afternoon. Only one was a failure — in

My stock soared to the skies.

Córdoba, Manolete's home town — where I was so very bad that they put me in jail! The next day I fought in Sevilla, "the cradle of bullfighting," the most fearsome plaza of all because the whole populace is so bull-crazy that 80 per cent of the male audience has tried fighting themselves at one time or another, and you can't fool them about anything to do with la fiesta brava.

As I paraded into the ring at the head of my cuadrilla and made the solemn bow to the presidente, a group of men rose up in the stands and said angrily, "Hey you, we've come down from Córdoba!"

I looked up and answered, "Well you've got a lot of guts to come see me after yesterday."

"That's the truth," they said, but some smiled.

I was pretty good on my first bull, and better on my second. However, while executing a difficult pass I got gored badly in the upper leg. My sword boy Vargas and Gago tried to drag me off to the infirmary; but I had dreamed of success in the "cradle of bullfighting" too long to leave my first performance there unfinished. I fought them off, picked up my sword and muleta, and managed to hobble out in front of the bull with the blood running down my leg. I could hear Gago saying, agonized, "No, Carlos, no!" as I shook the muleta to make the animal charge. As it came at me I hopped toward it on one leg, then reached over the lowered horns and sank the sword in up to the hilt. The bull dropped over and so did I. They carried me out, but I had the bull's ears in my hand — and the cheers of the world's finest aficionados ringing in my head.

So ended the 1944 season for me on September 28 — forty-four corridas in sixty days, the hardest and best of my life. But it was just the beginning.

10

Against Gago's advice, I left for Mexico as soon as I was well enough to travel. "Stay here this winter," he urged me. "Rest, train with the calves, and get ready for the spring season."

But no, I had a burning desire to be really good in Mexico City just once, a human failing, the urge to show off at home. I could hardly wait to show them my new style, and I looked forward to the warm reception the hometown boy would get after his triumphal season in Spain.

I should have listened to Gago. I was greeted with coldness and hostility on all sides in Mexico, for reasons I'll never understand. I suppose it was partly because I had refused to make the customary bribes to some of the bullfight critics, since I was attacked ferociously by the newspapers. Among other things they claimed I wasn't a real Mexican, since my parents were Spanish, and that, plus political reasons and bribery, accounted for my "moderate success in Spain." I tried to show them in the bullring, but my terrible luck in Mexico City persisted and I was like my old self rather than the new. The bulls were partly to blame, but it was also

WHAT DID YOU EXPECT FROM THESE DAGO'S MATADOR

that the frigidness I found toward me in the crowd right from the start of every corrida threw me off stride. Their attitude was: "Well, you've somehow managed to hoodwink those Spaniards, boy, but we've known you ever since you were a little pick-nose calf-fighter, so don't try any of your fancy fakery on us." TYPICAL PEASANT ATTITUDE

I was licked before I would even make the first nervous cape pass. I slunk back to Spain as soon as possible, bruised, my confidence shattered, and wondering just how good a torero I really was and how much had been luck the season before.

The whole bullfighting world seemed to be waiting for my first performance now in Spain, since, thanks to the cables about my season in Mexico, the atmosphere was highly charged. They were saying that I wasn't the same, that I'd gone to pieces in Mexico, and many other things. Even my faithful backers were a little uneasy. I knew I'd have to do everything in my power to show them they were wrong as quickly as possible. I'd have to do something slightly sensational on my first fight, which was to be held in Castellón de la Plana.

On the boat going over I had practiced daily and had begun to think about creating a new pass. In every standard pass with the muleta the cloth is offered to the bull while the man either holds the target even with his body or in front of it. Theoretically, the bull will always take the big expanse the cloth makes rather than charge the comparatively small target of the man's legs. However, I remembered seeing men get gored because they held the muleta still and moved their legs and the bulls, attracted by the movement, ignored the cloth for the man. Suppose that I took the muleta in my right hand and held it *behind* my body, just letting a small portion of the flannel show. If I made that small bit alluring enough while keeping my legs completely

still, could I make a bull hook at it and ignore my exposed
legs? After all, one flipped the capote behind one's body
for the gaonera pass, and while then the matador did have
that great protective expanse of cloth with the big cape
which he didn't have with the little muleta, the basic principle was still the same.

Manolete had made his manoletina pass by simply taking
an old pass of La Serna's and adding the business of catching
the corner of the muleta with the left hand behind the back.

The
manoletina.

If I could get away with this idea of mine it might be more sensational for the audience than the manoletina; for the torero I knew it would be the most dangerous pass ever attempted.

The audience in the plaza de toros of Castellón de la Plana seemed to be made up entirely of skeptics with a you've-got-to-show-me attitude; all my publicity and the high prices that were charged were beginning to react adversely. The people certainly didn't get their money's worth on the opening capework, since my verónicas — always the weakest part of my performances — were worse than usual, simply because I was nervous and trying too hard to please. With the muleta I gave them some of my best passes and they warmed up considerably, though I still felt a certain disappointment; they had hoped for something truly sensational. As I came over to the fence to change muletas at one point I heard a manoletista in the crowd shout, "How about a manoletina or two, boy!" and the crowd laughed, because a torero never does a rival's special pass.

I said to myself: I'll try to give you something better than that, my friend! You'll either see a spectacular pass or a spectacular goring. Taking the sword and muleta I went out to the center of the empty ring.

"Toro!" I yelled at the bull. When it charged I did three normal right-handed passes. At the end of the last one, I continued to swing the muleta but then held it behind my legs, running after the bull, crowding it so that I would be virtually on top of it when it wheeled for the next charge. I knew that part of my hope of getting away with this maneuver would be in quickly getting the muleta so close to the animal's face that he didn't really have much opportunity to see my legs and have a choice.

As the bull veered around I waited for it with my right arm holding the muleta awkwardly around my back, my entire body exposed to its charge. I knew this was the most dangerous maneuver I'd ever attempted when I saw it bearing down on me, because if I saw it meant to hook into me instead of the cloth there would be nothing I could do: with my arm bent this way there was no possible flaring out of the cloth while jumping back out of the way as one could on other passes that were obviously not going to turn out. So I just kept my legs still and wagged the small portion of muleta that showed on the other side of my legs and prayed that he wouldn't think it too insignificant a target and would hook for it. All of this happened in a split second, of course, but it seemed a week to me that the right horn was heading straight for my thigh. I went way up on my toes and sucked in my stomach and shoved the tip of the muleta in the bull's face and then after the horn passed my waist, I leaned up against the charging bull's body and felt its long muscular bulk ripple against my stomach for its entire length.

There were no cheers from the audience, just a gasp, because they didn't realize that this was a pass; they thought I had somehow been caught unawares with the muleta in this strange position and by some miracle I hadn't been tossed. I myself was so amazed it had turned out right that I was unnerved and couldn't bring myself to try it again. I gave some more standard passes, killed the bull, and went to the barrera.

"Good God," said Gago. "What happened to you out there? If you could only do that thing on purpose you'd have the greatest pass ever invented!"

They gave me ears and tail for that first bull, but I was out for everything today. So after a great beginning on my second bull, I again went out into the center of the ring and gave them another look at my new pass, only this time I did it twice to show them it was on purpose. I started to do it a

Leaned up against the charging bull's body.

third time, but even before I put the muleta behind me I realized I wouldn't get away with it, that the bull was catching on to the trick, so I went into a series of the more standard molinete pass. The crowd went absolutely wild. After I killed the animal they demanded that I be granted ears, tail, and hoof.

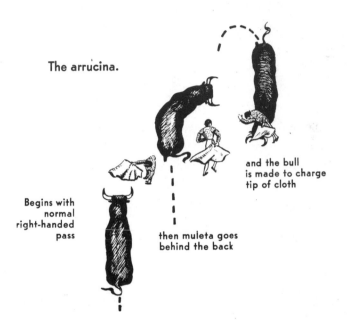

The arrucina.

and the bull
is made to charge
tip of cloth

Begins with
normal
right-handed
pass

then muleta goes
behind the back

And so I started out the best season of my life and so the arrucina was born.* There would be days when I would regret having had this idea, since word spread instantly all over Spain about the new pass. Everyone wanted to see it; but there were many bulls who made it impossible to do.

* The arrucina is probably still the most difficult pass to do in the arena, and few toreros even attempt it. It is a comforting thought on the rightness of things that no one has ever done it with the grace and facility of its inventor, just the way no one has ever done the manoletina like Manolete, the chicuelina like Chicuelo, and the gaonera like Gaona.

At least once an afternoon.

Usually, however, I could pull it off at least once an afternoon, and when I did the roar of surprise from the audience
was wonderful music to me.

The following corrida was in Barcelona, on the 2nd of
April, and I remember it as one of the most complete corridas
of my life. I was received with many demonstrations of
affection by the public, and it was in this fight that the last
traces of doubt that could have remained about the results
of my season in Mexico disappeared. I cut ears off both bulls,
plus the hoof off the second. I must mention that in this
fight was the best and bravest and most noble bull of all the
ones that I have ever fought or seen come out of a toril. He

was called "Inspector," weighed over 600 kilos,* and was fantastically brave from the first moment he galloped into the arena. It was a bull from the Carmen de Federico ranch, and the foreman of the ranch several days before the fight had gone to a photographer and said, "Be sure to take a photograph of this bull, because this is a *toro de bandera*" — a real flag bull, a bull with which history is made. The foreman was sad to see this bull go to the ring. He had said to it, "Good-bye, Inspector, I love you like I love the pupils of my eyes," and he actually cried when he saw it go into the stalls where it would wait for the opening trumpet. The breeder said, "Be brave, good bull, put up a fight that we will all be proud of, and I want to get a telegram on Monday saying, 'Inspector was given a lap around the ring.'"

Dead bulls that have put up an ordinary fight are dragged straight out of the ring fast, with the audience either booing or applauding according to the degree of bravery they displayed. Bulls of extraordinary bravery are dragged slowly around the ring once and then out.

Two slow laps around the ring was what Inspector got — and deserved. At the beginning of the fight he came into the arena and placed himself in the very center, as though to say, "Gentlemen, I am the master around here!" What a bull! When he started to charge it was impossible to stop him. I remember trying to end a very long series of muleta passes, but the noble animal wouldn't give me a chance to get away. Pass after pass after pass, including two arrucinas, and it was just a question of who was going to tire first, the bull or I. In the very first passes the audience, as one person, took their handkerchiefs out and began waving them for the ear to be granted to me. I felt like saying to the audience, "The bull's the one who should get the trophies today." He was so splendid and so noble that when the time for the

* Over 1300 pounds.

kill came I hated to do it; I kept hoping that the presidente would grant him a pardon.* But he didn't, so I took my sword and granted the bull the speediest death that it was in my power to give.

From Barcelona we went to fight in Viñaroz, Granada, and then on to Valencia. Some time before, a brave young Valencian boy had been killed by a bull. His name was Manolo Cortés and he had had tremendous promise because of his skill and courage. This is a dangerous game of ours, probably the most dangerous in the world. But considering how close to death the average matador comes every afternoon he fights, and considering how many almost-fatal gorings there are every season, there are comparatively few deaths, in terms of the risk.** So we never got hardened to it, especially when it comes to a young friend. I had known Manolo in Barcelona where I saw him fight a novillada. He had dedicated the bull to me and I went to see him afterwards to congratulate him. Never have I seen such a polite, decent, serious young boy. We became good friends in the short time I knew him. I felt very badly when I learned how a bull had ripped out his life, and I decided that the first time I fought in his home town I would turn over the proceeds to his mother. I mention this only to explain the

* Very rarely, when a bull is incredibly brave, it will be granted the *indulto* — a pardon — and be turned out to stud. There have been many famous such bulls, but probably the most renowned was Civilón, a Cobaleda bull, who was fought in Barcelona in 1936. Although extremely brave, when his breeder called him halfway through the fight he trotted over docilely and allowed himself to be petted. After he was pardoned, the matador, El Estudiante, visited him and was able to lean casually on the animal which a short time before was trying to kill him. Civilón's ultimate fate was to be killed and eaten by soldiers in the civil war.

** Of the 113 major matadors since 1700, 41 have been killed. Besides these a great many minor though legitimate full matadors have died in the ring. There have been 111 recorded deaths of official novilleros, such as Manolo Cortés, since 1786, but there must have been almost that many unrecorded aspirants killed; 57 picadors and 118 banderilleros are listed fatalities since the middle of the 19th century.

fantastic welcome I got in Valencia, considering I'd never even fought there. There were banners across the streets, bands, and welcoming committees.

This demonstration actually made my task that much harder, because I certainly didn't want people to think this was a publicity stunt; I wanted to earn my applause out in front of the bulls, and not get it as a reward for a gesture. As it turned out, I drew good bulls and cut four ears and a tail, and I remember with amusement and pleasure how a few days later, upon my leaving a café, some aficionados spotted me and without so much as a how-do-you-do they picked me up on their shoulders and carried me all the way to my hotel!

After that corrida Gago came to me and said: "How many corridas do you feel up to fighting this season?"

"The more the merrier," I answered cheerily. I was on top of the world, in perfect condition, and I wanted all the performances I could get; it was as though I were terrified that there might remain someone in the world who wouldn't see me while this lucky streak was upon me.

"Well," said Gago quietly, "I'm glad you feel that way. You see, I've signed you for ninety-five corridas."

Ninety-five corridas! The most Manolete had ever fought in a single season was ninety-three.

"And if you keep up like this," said Gago, "we'll probably be offered another fifty. If you think you're up to it."

"Fine," said I in my cocky ignorance. "Take everything we can get!"

The next fight was Murcia, where I appeared with Manolete. The rivalry was again played up by the newspapers, and we were both out to give the other one "the bath." As it turned out it was a tie, with both of us cutting the same number of ears. The rival factions in the stands had to settle which one of their favorites had been better by fistfights after the performance. I still hadn't spoken to the Monster of Córdoba, nor he to me. If our glances crossed as we were waiting in the courtyard for the opening trumpet, it was more likely to be a glare on my part. He looked as though he was too tired and bored even to work up a glare, so he generally just looked through me vacantly.

Even after the second fight at the Sevilla fair, when the bulls tossed both of us and we emerged with our uniforms in shreds, we still didn't speak. He was tossed in a frightening fashion and it was a shocking thing, because he looked so completely invulnerable and secure that I didn't quite believe any bull could do that to him. It seemed almost like sacrilege when the bull flung him ten feet in the air and then tried to get a horn into his skinny body as he lay on the sand. I was the first to get out there with my cape and lure the bull away from the fallen man, and, enemies or not, I remember how glad I felt inside when he lurched to his feet and I saw that he wasn't injured. I started to tell him I was pleased that he hadn't been hurt; at the same time, it seemed to me, he looked as though he might be about to say

It was a
shocking thing.

The constant
wearing movement.

something, perhaps thanks to me for having made the *quite*,
but at that moment the bull began to head toward us and
there was no time. At the next fight's beginning we came
together before the parade with the same aloofness and
mutual dislike.

The season was beginning to take on a blurry, frantic
pattern now. One fight after another, the constant wearing
movement, hurrying from car or plane to hotel, from hotel
to bullring, from the bullring to the station wagon and the
highway again. To say nothing of the constant tension of
the threat of the bulls and the crowds! I had a superb
custom-made Buick station wagon whose back part could
convert to a bed. Sometimes one of my banderilleros drove

and I would snatch some sleep, but generally I was too keyed up to sleep and preferred to drive myself. It seemed to relax me. I actually began to get blisters on my hands from hauling on the steering wheel over Spain's winding roads, and very definitely had blisters in another place as well. Cerrillo and Aguilar were the greatest of companions, however, and they made the long trips seem shorter. I bought myself a guitar and anyone could tell the triumphal afternoons by the singing. When things didn't turn out so well the guitar remained as silent as a cadaver. Fortunately it got played quite a bit. But soon, even following an afternoon when a hoof was cut, I was too weary to pluck a guitar string. Little by little I began to see why Manolete looked so tired and old. This was a pace to kill a man.

When Gago came in one day to the hotel room as I was dressing and said jubilantly, "We've now signed for 154 fights this season!" I gave a groan and said, "Fine, you fight them."

"Don't think you can handle it? I could cancel some."

Reason told me that this number of fights would kill me. But that eternal drive of mine wouldn't let me alone. "We'll fight them all," I said.

On the 9th of May in Valencia, Parrita, Manolete, and I had a historic fight. There were twelve ears, six tails, and three hoofs cut off those six bulls that afternoon by the three of us. We divided the trophies equally, and the next day the papers referred to the bullring as *un manicomio* — an insane asylum — because of the audience's reaction.

The next day I had a greater and more satisyfing success. The impresario organized a party in the back part of the bullring, in the courtyard by the corrals, and the three matadors were invited as guests of honor. Deliberately, diabolically, they seated Manolete and me next to each other. I guess they just wanted to see the fireworks when the two enemies got together. At the beginning everything was serious, very cold, and completely silent. I nodded to him, however, and he nodded back. This, considering our past salutations, was practically the equivalent to an affectionate embrace.

Then something happened. I don't know even now how we started. It was something simple like "They call this food?" — but it broke the ice, and all of a sudden Manolete and I were talking.

"You missed a fine opportunity to let me get killed off there in Sevilla," he said laconically. "I've wanted to thank you for not doing it."

"What would I do for a rival then?" I joked back off-handedly. "I need the stimulus of the little competition you give me."

Then I saw something I thought was impossible. His mouth widened and he gave a low rumbling noise. Manolete was laughing! Then we began, and we talked and laughed steadily all through the meal and stayed on afterwards for another hour. We would have stayed all afternoon but we both had fights in other cities, and so after a warm handshake we said good-bye until our next fight together.

That was how I began to know Manolete, the other Manolete, the charming, friendly, humorous one who existed only away from the plaza de toros. I had never met anyone whom I liked and admired so much as this man to whom bullfighting was a religion.

At first many people around us didn't like the idea of our being friends. They thought that our hate for one another was the motive for our going out there to work so close to the bull every day, and that once friends the rivalry would end. But that impression did not last long, since our first ring duels after that friendly meeting were perhaps more intense than before.

Never have I seen a more noble companion than Manolo (as his intimates called him), nor anyone more fierce and jealous of his name and reputation. Yet many times after having cut ears and tail off his bull he would come over just before my bull came out and say in his deep, serious voice, "Come on now, Carlos, don't make me look like a complete villain — I'd like to see you with the ears of this bull in your hands."

"Anything to oblige, Manolo," I'd say to him, and if I managed to cut the ears, how pleased he would look.

We went along like this in perfect harmony, fighting together almost daily and appreciating each other more and more, but never letting anybody notice it inside the arena. Away from the ring we became like brothers, but inside the ring it was each man for himself.

I had never met anyone whom I liked and admired so much as this man.

Inside the ring it was each man for himself.

11

GAGO CAME into my hotel room happily. "We're going to make bullfighting history," he said.

"How?" I asked suspiciously. I had come to be a little wary of Gago's projects because they usually involved his risking my neck.

"You're going to fight in Madrid!"

"What's so historical about that — I fought there last year."

"Ah yes, but with animals that were barely weaned. This time it will be with bulls — real bulls!"

The way he said it made my blood grow cold. "You mean those monsters I fought there last year weren't big enough for you?"

"Nothing! Wait till you see what I've got lined up — they'll scare the audience to death."

"What about the toreros?"

"When you triumph with these bulls, you'll go down as one of the greatest toreros of all time."

I argued with him, saying it wasn't worth the risk of having a flop and that I should play it safe with a more comfortable type of animal.

Manolete and I were both in such demand now that at any time we could state, "We won't fight unless we can go out to the ranches and pick out the bulls ourselves." We wouldn't actually pick out the particular two bulls that we were going to fight that afternoon, but we would select six bulls to make sure that they were all of the same caliber and with no defects and not too big. It's very tempting for a top bull-fighter to abuse and overwork this privilege, and it is a normal reaction, since just taking whatever the impresario and breeder decide to push off on you can be a harrowing part of a bullfighter's life.

Gago, however, didn't see things my way, especially since Manolete had received some criticism from the press a few days before for fighting a "too comfortable" group of bulls. If I were to make my first fight in Madrid this year with tremendous bulls from one of the most dangerous of the ranches, my stock would rise considerably. And so it was that my presentation was announced with six bulls of Pablo Romero, for the 24th of May.

Along with the Miura bulls, Pablo Romeros are the most feared of Spain. They are always the largest bulls fought in the season, and bullfighters with any sense at all try to avoid them. Certainly no one in his right mind would choose to fight an important fight like a presentation in Madrid with such difficult animals.

That I was going to fight with these bulls created a great stir in the *afición* throughout Spain. But Gago was right, because it was a stroke of genius. I say it now, now that it's all over, but I certainly wasn't thinking along those lines the eve before the fight, since I was very "nervous." There was a complete sellout three days before the fight, and all Madrid seemed to be divided into two camps, one saying that I probably could repeat what they'd read that I had been doing in the provinces, and the other saying that they'd really see me fail with these bulls that were the size of the bulls that used to be fought fifty years ago.

A fine little package Gago had wrapped up for me! Before going in the arena the next day I kept telling myself, Look, these are animals just like any other, so just forget their name and size and go out there and do your best, just as though this were in Valencia or Murcia with ordinary bulls.

On my first animal, an angry mountain of black and white muscle, I managed to do well enough so that I got a lap around the ring. A lap around the ring in Madrid is the equivalent of both ears in any other bullring in Spain. But still I wanted to do something better, something very special and sensational. The animal hadn't been right to try an arrucina on, since he had a bad left hook and that is the only side on which an arrucina can be done. So when my second bull came out, even larger than the first, I resolved to give the public of Madrid a look at my new pass. I quickly saw to my dismay that this animal had exactly the same defect as the first.

As Vargas handed me the muleta and sword, a drunk who had been heckling me all through the fight called down from the first row: "Listen, you clown, that telephone business they say you did once, let's just see you try that here with *this* animal!"

He was referring to an adorno I had tried in Valladolid. In a book once I had seen an old print of a bullfighter named Reverte, who was supposed to have rested his elbow on a bull's forehead and got away with it. This had stuck in my mind. When I drew a rather sedentary small bull in Valladolid, at one point in the fight when I felt the animal wouldn't be likely to charge, I leaned forward and gingerly rested my elbow between its horns. It created quite a sensation and the papers referred to it as El Teléfono.

Now as I went out with this giant Pablo Romero I thought

Reverte doing the first "teléfono" around 1900.

Arruza's version in 1945.

how it would bring the house down if I could pull it off again. I waited until the middle of the faena, until I had the animal under control and dominated by the muleta. Then, after a series of right-handed passes, I saw that the bull was momentarily confused. I turned suddenly, slipped down to my knees right in his face, and, leaning forward, I planted my elbow on the curly hair between his horns as the crowd watched in disbelief. The bull itself seemed too astonished to charge and let me get away with this impertinence. Then I got up and killed the bull with one thrust. When I walked back to the barrera I smiled up very sweetly to that good gentleman and said, "At your service, señor."

And so the days went by like this, one hurdle after another had to be overcome, fight after fight, city after city, and nearly always with the fine companionship and terrible competition of Manolete. I liked the feeling of being in the arena with Manolo, because of the complete sense of mastery and security and even safety that he imparted to everyone. But one day in Alicante, while executing one of his perfect naturals, he worked in a centimeter too close to the horn. He was tossed very high and suffered a bad fracture of the clavicle when he hit the ground. I hurriedly finished off my last bull and went to see him in the infirmary. The doctors said he should be taken to Madrid immediately, so I sent the cuadrilla off in the station wagon and put Manolete in the back seat of my convertible. Then I set off with Pepe Bienvenida, the matador, to help spell me during the long drive. We had Manolete propped up with all kinds of cushions, but still the ride must have been agonizing. I glanced in the mirror from time to time and saw his sweaty pale face twist in agony as we went over the rough roads, swerving to avoid herds of animals, but he never complained. Pepe passed him back a flask of brandy.

A bad fracture
of the clavicle.

"If you're sure it's on you, I'll have one," Manolo said.

As I took a corner too fast and almost hit a tree, I heard Manolo suck in his breath in pain, but he merely gave a laugh and said between clenched teeth, "It's too bad this man can't work as close to the horns as he does to trees."

What a *man* he was!

We arrived in Madrid at dawn, where the doctors were waiting for Manolo. I went to my hotel and fell into bed, dead with fatigue and strain. Luckily I wasn't fighting the next day. At last — one whole day free to do nothing but sleep! What a marvelous feeling to collapse into a real bed and know you could sleep for twenty-four hours.

I hadn't been asleep for two hours when I felt Gago shaking me awake. He was there with the impresario from Segovia, who wanted me to substitute for Manolete in the Segovia plaza. I groaned and covered my head with the pillow. The man begged and explained what a terrible spot he was in, how he'd lose a fortune if he had to refund all the money, and so forth.

"But Andrés, I'm really exhausted," I said to Gago groggily. "I can hardly move!"

But I got dressed, went to see how Manolete was, and took off for Segovia. The doctors scared me when they told me that by a miracle Manolete hadn't been killed. It seems that a bone from the clavicle had splintered up toward his neck, and if we had hit a really bad bump on the road, Manolete wouldn't have been there. That's how I left him, all in plaster, and sad. I can still see his face as he wished me luck with one of his characteristic tragic smiles.

I had a good afternoon, with ears and tail off both bulls, but I also got the roughest blow that any bull has ever given me. My second bull hooked me and had me for a whole eternity on its horns without anybody's being able to get me off. It was Andrés Gago who jumped into the ring without a cape or anything else and grabbed me by my legs to drag me out from under the animal. Luckily, aside from the tremendous shaking up and the complete shredding of my uniform, nothing more serious happened.

People always ask me, "What do you think about in a

There's very little time for much profound thinking.

predicament like that?" Actually there's very little time for much profound thinking when you're up in the air on a bull's horn. Your thoughts are kaleidoscopic and nightmarish of course, but you're too busy working to try to fight the horn away from your flesh to be really scared. It's after the fight when you get scared about what happened — or when you see the movies and see how close it was.*

But after that escape I went to Burgos and there a bull, a Pablo Romero bull, really did get me, ripping a rather handsome wound up into my groin. It was my first bull, and my very first cape pass, and I don't even know how it happened, I just felt the animal slam into me, the horn rip up into my flesh, and there I was in the infirmary. It was as though

* A few months ago Arruza was watching the bullfighting movies in the bistro El Matador in San Francisco, some of him fighting very closely. He kept saying to himself in English: "Look out, Charlie, you're going to get hurt, you're going to get hurt!" When the film finally did show him getting tossed, he slumped down in his chair and said unhappily, "I tol' you so, you crazy fool."

Manolete and I had had an agreement: two days after his wounding I went to keep him company in the hospital.

I never thought that I'd be so glad to get to a hospital. How wonderful it was in there, just lying there resting, sleeping, and not having to fight bulls in the afternoon! I wanted to stay there for ever. Finally I had to leave, though, because awaiting me once again was the constant battle of la fiesta, and now I had a new problem — to demonstrate that the wound hadn't destroyed my spirit. Spaniards claim that a man loses his brave blood first, and I had to show them that this wasn't true.

Day after day I had to prove this. But my luck still held out. For example, in the feria of Valencia, which lasted seven days, I fought every single day, and cut nineteen ears, four tails, and two hoofs off my fourteen bulls. I couldn't ask for anything better. But I was beginning to get sick from so much bullfighting. Very seldom now did I get to sleep in a real bed. In one month I fought twenty-eight corridas out of the thirty days, and even at that I lost one because of a

Arruza rests his eyebrow on a horn and wins a hoof in Valencia.

slight wound that I suffered in Albacete. Because of this wound I thought I'd get in a longed-for rest of three or four days when I arrived at Madrid. But then I heard that my banderilleros Aguilar and Cerrillo and my picador Chavitos were starting out on a colossal drunk to enjoy themselves a little after so much fighting. When toreros go on a tear they do a complete and prolonged and masterful job of it. My God, how I wanted that rest! I knew, though, that if once we let down, we'd all go to pieces, and I needed that expert team. I had to head off the disaster. So, hardly able to move, I called them to me.

"Get everything ready," I said, "and let Valladolid know that we're fighting there tomorrow!" I bought myself a rubber ring to sit on in the station wagon, and off we went to Valladolid. Once again we started the terrible bruising schedule of fight after fight after fight.

But it was getting harder and harder for me to stand it. More than the actual fighting itself, which God knows was hard enough, what was wearing me down was the constant travel, the lack of sleep and rest, and always eating on the run in order to arrive on time from one bullring to another. Every night now, we would eat nothing more than a little box lunch in the station wagon as we drove, which Vargas, the sword boy, had prepared for us in the morning.

Then I had another accident. One of my hands was wounded in the plaza of Manzanares, because of which I lost fifteen corridas. I spent these wonderful days on the estate of Santa Coloma, doing nothing but resting, resting, resting.*

It was during that period that I was accorded the great honor of being invited to preside over a corrida as a judge along with those two immortals and all-time maestros, Rafael

---

* Maybe that was Carlos' idea of resting; I distinctly remember his coming around to the American Consulate several times to pick me up, and we went out to the ranches and fought calves for diversion and then went out all night on the town. He was just too wound up really to relax.

Juan Belmonte, Rafael "El Gallo," and Arruza.

"El Gallo" and Juan Belmonte. I believe this did as much as anything to convince me that I had really arrived in the bull world.

How wonderful that layoff was, because when I reappeared I seemed like a new man. Once again, however, the daily bullfighting began to leave me as thin as a candlewick. There were times when Cerrillo had to wake me up in the very gate leading to the ring, since I just went to sleep there standing up. When we would arrive back of the ring of any plaza, and while we were waiting for the affair to begin, I would immediately move away from the others and lean up against the wall, and my men would see to it that I wasn't bothered for photos or autographs or anything for a few minutes while I grabbed a little sleep. Then the trumpet would blow and Cerrillo would come over and shake me by the shoulder and say, "Come on, Carlos, time for the party." Then mechanically I would step out into the ring like a sleepwalker and make the parade. I wouldn't truly wake up until the toril gate was flung open and the bull came out into the ring. I remember once how a young torero came up to introduce himself, but I was too groggy and didn't know his name and didn't arouse myself until too late, and I thought of how I had reacted to the same treatment with Manolete so long ago.

This was the physical state I was in when I fought my best fight, the best fight of my life, in Málaga, on the 27th of August. They were offering a beautiful medallion to the bullfighter who put up the best display in the three-day fair. I promised the medallion to my mother, and I wanted to win it badly. I did, and she still wears it.

⠿ ⠿   TRANSLATOR'S NOTE

I CAN'T let Arruza get away with dismissing this now historic fight so easily. Since I was in on it peripherally, I must go into it in more detail for you.

In an essay on la fiesta brava in the *Journal of Esthetics,* Patricia Hetter has written so very well:

The ideal bullfight, as it has been described, exists only in the imagination. It is an ideal which the aficionado carries in his head and he will be fortunate if he sees the ideal approached more than a few times in his lifetime.

Thus he attends every Sunday afternoon in the season, drawn by the hope — not even an expectation — of seeing the theoretical corrida realized. Moreover, when the corrida falls very far short of theory, it is a brutal and degrading spectacle. Only a hair divides tragedy from travesty. Thus this particular aesthetic experience cannot be predicted. A concert-goer carefully calculates the quality of his pleasure beforehand. He has the program, the reputation of the con-

ductor, and of the orchestra, perhaps past experience with both, to guide him. The aficionado may know the matador, but there are too many variables for him to know the serene expectancy of the concert-goer. No one can gauge the stature of a bull in advance of his actual trial, and the tragedy, once begun, must go on to the end, no matter how recalcitrant the bull or reluctant the matador. On such an occasion, beauty evaporates like a curtain of mist, exposing the pain and cruelty for which beauty is the only apologist.

Since attending my first corrida when I was thirteen, I have seen hundreds and hundreds of bullfights, some of them excellent, many fair, most of them bad. But of all of them I have seen the ideal realized only these times:

Juan Belmonte with his one bull at Castillo de la Guardas, Spain, in September, 1945, when, at the age of fifty-five he demonstrated how will can triumph over physical limitations and even age.

Manolete in Barcelona in the fall of the same year. After having been piqued by a spectator's bellowing "Better watch out — Arruza's coming!" Manolete glanced up and rumbled: "Que venga — let him come!" And then he went out with both his bulls to show us what a truly sublime, regal, cool, perfect machine he was.

Luis Procuna in Peru in 1946, when he was almost booed out of the ring for his cowardly and insulting performance on his first bull, a good one, and then came back with the last bull of the afternoon, a treacherous buffalo, to show Armillita, Manolete, and the rest of the onlookers the most startling and emotional faena Lima had ever seen.

Cañitas in Málaga, Spain, on August 26, 1945, when, in the competition for the award for the best performance of the annual fair, he arose to artistic heights he didn't know were in him.

Juan Belmonte

The
Perfect
Ones

Procuna

Manuel Rodríguez, "Manolete"

Carlos Vera, "Cañitas"

But best of all, without a doubt, was Arruza, in Málaga, on August 27, 1945. The man was twenty-five and the bull was five, just as the great Guerrita said it should be.

It's a good story and a true one, one that I've used as a basis for fictional tales. I might do well to tell in detail what can happen when all the elements that go into making la fiesta brava come off right. Maybe it will show how and why Arruza became such a hero to the Spaniards. Maybe it will help to convey what Hemingway calls "that emotional and spiritual intensity and pure, classic beauty that can be produced by a man and a bull and a piece of scarlet serge draped over a stick."

I had a fine big house in Málaga and I was known as a friend of Arruza's, so that's why the Town Council came to me. "Mire, Señor Vice-Consul," they said. "We are going to present a gorgeous diamond medallion to the torero who gives the best performance at the bullfights during our annual fair. It is an exquisite thing, made especially in Madrid, at a cost of 9000 pesetas, and we should enjoy the honor of presenting it to your friend Arruza in your house."

"The honor will be mine," I said. "And I shall plan a party for that date. But how can you be sure Arruza will put up the best show?"

"He cannot fail," they said. "First: he is fighting both Friday and Sunday; if he is out of form or the bulls are bad on Friday, he will have another chance on Sunday. And secondly, Manolete, Arruza's only real competition, has been wounded and will not be able to fight."

"And thirdly," spoke up the little treasurer uneasily, "he has to be the best, for we already have his name engraved on the medallion!"

On Friday Carlos arrived for the first fight and Málaga was agog, because he had become the most sensational thing in bullfighting. When I went to see him the afternoon of the fight his face was pale and drawn and I could see that the eighty fights he had already fought under this regime had aged him.

"Chiquillo," he said after we'd talked awhile and he wiggled into the gold-brocaded pants, "what's this about a medallion?"

I explained.

"Caracoles!" exclaimed Carlos. "They've put my name on it already! But anything can happen in a bullfight! How can they know if I feel like fighting? Or what about the wind? Or what about the bulls, eh? That slight detail must be considered — the bulls."

At four o'clock they paraded into the brilliant sun and the band blared forth with the pasodoble, "Carlos Arruza." Carlos grinned nervously and threw his dress cape up to me.

His first bull was a bad one, but he did pretty well, and the presidente let him take a lap around the ring to receive the crowd's applause. The second bull was the matador Estudiante's and he did a very good job, being conceded two ears from the dead animal as an evaluation of his bravery and skill. Morenito de Talavera felt the pressure of the two good fights that had gone before him, and surpassed by far his natural ability, cutting one ear and taking a lap around the ring.

Arruza, seemingly unconcerned by this competition as he waited for his second bull to come out, looked around, hugging his big red and yellow cape to him and smiling his little-boy smile at friends.

His bull skidded out of the toril and brought some boos from the crowd because it was so small. But the boos switched to olé's when Arruza passed the bull closely three times, the lethal horns inches away from his knees. Few people objected when, after he had placed three beautifully executed pairs of banderillas, dedicated the bull to the

1

5

9

Aruzza placing banderillas in Málaga, August 25, 1945.

3

4

7

8

11

12

glamorous gypsy singer Lola Flores, and dispatched the bull with one sword thrust, the presidente granted him both ears and the tail. Women threw down roses to him and men threw cigars, hats, even overcoats. A few people booed, though, saying he didn't deserve the tail, since the bull was so small.

However, the medal seemed cinched, especially after Estudiante and Morenito de Talavera were bad on the last two bulls, and I left the plaza jubilantly. The next day the program was Estudiante and Morenito again plus a little Mexican Indian named Cañitas. Nothing to fear, we thought, for the bulls were giants; we had seen what Estudiante and Morenito had to offer, and who ever heard of Cañitas? An ugly little Indian who had been around Mexico for years, he was a competent, brave craftsman, but hardly in the same league with Arruza.

None of the three fighters was anything but discreet on his first bull. But then the trumpet sounded for Cañitas second. Out it came — a black and white monster weighing 750 kilos!*

Cañitas went pale when he saw the creature rip a section of the wooden barrier apart, but he set his Indian jaw and you could see him telling himself, "If I'm going to die I'll go out in a blaze of glory!" The bull ran around the empty ring twice looking for something to kill, and then Cañitas stepped out and dropped to his knees, letting it go by with a *whoosh,* as the great horns passed his head. A gasp of surprise went up from the crowd, who expected him to play the bull as safely as possible. Then when he passed the bull even closer, they set up a continuous roar. After numerous fancy passes with the cape, he placed three sets of banderillas with the arrogance of a gypsy, he accomplished a faena with the muleta that bullfighters dream about, and then drew back

* Almost 1700 pounds.

and dropped the bull with a sword thrust to the hilt. The crowd went wild and insisted upon his getting both ears, tail, and a hoof, the most you can possibly get. I left the plaza for the day, feeling a little sick.

The next day was Sunday, and the Town Council came to see me with long faces. "Now what do we do?" they asked reproachfully, as though it were my fault. "Order another medallion," was all I could suggest.

Arruza arrived at six in the morning, after having fought in Puerto de Santa María the afternoon before and driving all night to Málaga. I went to the hotel to awake him at three. The idol of Spain was a mess; he looked green, and staggered as he got up.

"I'm exhausted." The words tumbled out. "I've a fever of 102; I can't go on like this every day. I never want to fight again. I'm going to go to bed for ten years when the season is over. How was the fight yesterday?" Wearily he put on his frilled shirt. "I haven't seen the papers yet."

"Cañitas turned in the best fight of the season," I said.

Carlos stopped tying his tie. "Are you joking?"

It was no secret that he and Cañitas had thoroughly disliked each other for years.

"No," I said. "He got inspired — fought as he's never fought before — cut ears, tail — and a hoof!" I cleared my throat. "But — uh —you'll come up to the house for the ceremony anyway, won't you?"

Arruza regarded me quietly and said, "I'll be there, chiquillo."

I think for the first time I felt the tremendous will and iron determination of this man emanate from him. Under his pleasant, easy exterior he had a fierce, gnawing inability to allow himself to be second best to anybody in the world.

I made the error of taking two women to the last fight. Carlos was first on the program, and when he got to his

Carlos did every pass in the book.

knees and let the bull pass by him four times so close that it removed part of his embroidered jacket, the girl on my right passed out; the other girl was about to faint also, but she was too busy reviving her friend. Carlos did every pass in the book, plus two of his own invention, and the girls couldn't stand any more. They left just about the time he dropped the bull with one thrust. The crowd went wild, and the presidente signaled with his handkerchief for the banderillero to cut one ear, then the other. Next he signaled for the tail, and finally the hoof, and Arruza circled the ring, triumphantly, holding his prizes aloft.

It was a wonderful fight, a great fight, and we were limp from the emotion of it. But we all knew in our hearts that Cañitas had been just a bit more reckless, more daring, more suicidal the day before.

After Arruza, came Parrita and Andaluz, both good bullfighters, but people were still groggy from the first fight and didn't pay any attention to them. When Arruza came out and stood there swaying, waiting for his second bull people applauded wildly, but we really didn't expect him to do anything more today. It is rare when a bullfighter is able to put up good performances on both bulls, much less great ones.

The trumpet blew, the torilero jerked the rope that clanged open the heavy Gate of Frights, and out blasted the bull. It was a monstrous creature from Villamarta. Arruza studied it as it charged viciously against a burladero and sent the top slats splintering into the air. Carlos was pale and looked as though he might throw up, but when one of his banderilleros started to go out to give it some testing passes, Arruza waved him back with a cut of his hand.

"Tápate!" he ordered. "Hide yourself!"

Carlos stepped out shakily into the ring and stood there swaying. He put his hand to his feverish head and pressed his hot temples. It looked as though he might faint. But then when the bull spotted him and lowered his head and started across the ring toward him, he collected himself. Taking the cape in one hand, he dropped to his knees.

"Toro," he called, swirling the cape out flat on the sand in front of him. And then I remember he called in a casual, invitational, mocking tone, "Eh, toro, why don't you try charging around this way?"

As the bull thundered down on him Arruza watched it come, his face resigned, as though saying: "Maybe you'll crash into my chest but I'm down here on my knees now and it's restful and I really don't feel well enough to get up and jump out of the way."

When the bull was four feet away, Arruza suddenly swung the cape over his head, flashing it from the left side over to the right. The bull veered off its course after the flare of cloth, and the animal's right horn grazed by Arruza's right eye.

A roar came from the crowd and then more roars as Arruza stayed there on his knees and did five liquid, fantastic faroles, so close that each time cape and man and bull made a beautiful blurry tangle of gold and black and magenta.

By the time the banderillas act came around the plaza was already a sea of white handkerchiefs demanding ears for the matador even if he did nothing else for the rest of the fight. Then Carlos placed the three greatest pairs of barbed sticks I've ever seen, running at an angle at the bull as it charged, and sticking them in the withers with his arms high, his chest only inches from the horns, and finally spinning to one side to let the bull hurtle by. He begged permission from the presidente to risk his life in still another pair. It was granted, and Carlos picked an impossible way to place them: with his back against the fence, he incited the bull, "Uh-huh, toro! Uh-huh-huh!" and stood there calmly watching it bear down on him. When the animal was two feet away, Carlos raised his arms, dropped the banderillas in place, ducked to the side, the left horn grazing his waist as the bull crashed into the fence.

The trumpet blew for the death; with the scarlet rag and the curved sword in his hand, Carlos dedicated the bull, facing the crowd with exhausted, unseeing eyes. Then he went out for the last round.

His first pass with the muleta was the regal, dangerous Pass of Death. Carlos called the bull from twenty feet away, and as it *whooshed* by he remained absolutely motionless and straight, letting the bull choose whether he was going to crash into the cloth or into his legs. Still motionless, and without even looking at the animal, he let the bull wheel and charge again. And then again and again and still again, without moving an inch. Nine times he willed that bull into taking the cloth instead of his body, and nine times he should have been killed. By this time there were no *olé*'s from the

Motionless,
and without
even looking
at the animal.

But the bull
was already
charging.

audience, only wild gobblings and hoarse croaks and cries of "Oh God, oh God!"

Then he decided to show the crowd his invention — the arrucina. When he flipped the muleta around behind his back and offered the bull only the small corner of the cloth that protruded, and the audience realized what he was going to try to do, they began to chant, "No, no, no!"

But the bull was already charging. Carlos went up on his toes, his stomach sucked in and as the horn knifed by, it caught on the inside of his jacket and ripped it open. But he wasn't hit. He immediately crowded the bull, the muleta still behind him and cited the animal for another arrucina again. This time the bull got only halfway through the charge before lunging to the left.

The crowd screamed as Arruza went up into the air, not high but clutching on to the horns of the animal, clinging to its tossing head, and then spinning on the right horn. Somehow when his body slapped the ground, he was stretched out under the bull, the length of his body between the animal's front legs, and his head between the lowered horns. People hid their eyes, for there was no time for his helpers to get there and lure the bull off him.

Before the points could find the inert form, Carlos reached up and locked his arms around the bull's neck in a frantic grip. The bewildered bull spun around and around. Finally it gave its neck a great snap, and flung the man from him like a rag doll to the ground ten feet away. But before it could charge, Arruza's men were between them and attracted the bull's attention. Arruza lurched drunkenly to his feet and stood there swaying, bruised and dazed, his uniform jacket in ribbons, but miraculously not wounded. He picked up his sword and the rag.

"Fuera!" he yelled at his banderilleros. "Get out of the ring."

This is a customary theatrical gesture from matadors who have been tossed, but it is never taken seriously and the men stayed in the ring, ready for any emergency. Arruza repeated it.

"Fuera!"

The amazed men retreated several feet behind him.

Arruza whirled on them and snarled, "Fuera, I said! Leave me alone with him!"

When they had all left the ring, the matador turned to the bull, who was pawing the ground and studying him ten feet away. Carlos dropped to his knees. He stared into the bull's hot eyes. Then he began to inch forward toward the animal. Closer and closer he came. The bull shifted his feet and the crowd gasped, sure that it would charge. But it didn't; it was as though it were hypnotized and cowed by the enormous brute courage of this man-thing on its knees. Arruza kept coming, and coming, and coming, staring fixedly at the bull until he arrived at its very face.

Then, with the muzzle of the bull almost touching him, he leaned forward and rested his elbow on the bull's fore-

head! Then he rested his own forehead on the bull's right horn! Then he took the horn tip in his teeth! A sudden lunge and the horn would have been spiked out through the back of the man's head.

He turned around and stared up at the crowd with the bull's nose against his back, a horn jutting out on either side of his head. We were afraid to scream for fear the noise would make the bull charge, but when he faced the bull again and, still on his knees, made it pass by four times, spinning in against the shoulder each time, a great roar burst from our throats. And then suddenly Carlos rose to his feet. He hurled himself between the horns, sank the sword in the shoulders to the hilt, and the bull only had time to cough once before it reeled, and crashed over backward to the sand, dead.

Delirium took over the plaza. The presidente waved his handkerchief for one ear, again for two ears, again for the tail, again for a hoof — and still again for another hoof, for the first time in bullfighting's long history But still the crowd kept chanting, "Más, y más, y más!" — more, more, more! Finally, as it kept up and kept up, the presidente just shrugged and said, "Hell, take the whole bull then."

So Arruza got the medal and we had the party, and what a party it was; but our honored guest left at midnight.

He had to hurry to Logroño for a fight the following day.

🐂 🐂

LITTLE BY LITTLE, the end of the season was approaching, with me fighting every day. But one day, the 7th of October, I just couldn't go on. I was fighting in Valencia, a *mano a mano* between Manolete and myself, which turned out wonderfully well, and right in the middle of it I turned to Andrés and said, "Cancel everything — I just can't fight one more bull — I just can't do it." Andrés* saw what bad shape I was in and my season in Spain for that year was finished.

The final results were: I had signed for 154 corridas in Spain. I had fought 108. Plus that were the four fights in Mexico, which made it a total for the year of 112, plus four benefit festival fights. Of those 232 bulls I killed, I placed banderillas in 190 of them, and from them I managed to harvest 219 ears, 74 tails, and 20 hoofs. ** I am proud to say that in the majority of these fights I performed side by side with Manolete.

But I was tired, terribly hollow, numb, sick-tired, and I felt like resting for ever. Yet, somehow, incredibly, after sleeping for a week, I found myself accepting contracts to go to Peru, Colombia, and Venezuela. I left Spain shortly for the grinding pace in those countries where Manolete and I would once more continue our hard competition. The drive was still compelling me.

* Gago says Arruza could have forced himself to fight one or two more fights, but that the real reason for his quitting was that in 1919 Carlos' idol, Juan Belmonte, set up a record which had never been beaten, that of fighting 109 corridas in a single season in Spain; out of respect he didn't want to equal or better it.

** Thus Arruza sums up what must be the most brilliant single season that any bullfighter has had in the history of the spectacle.

12

Now it was the summer of 1947 and I was forced to limit myself to Portuguese and French plazas, because the breaking of the bullfighting agreement again prevented us Mexicans from performing in Spain. I had two corridas signed for the 27th and 28th of August in the plaza of Dax in France, so we set out from Sevilla in the station wagon and on the way stopped at San Sebastian, where the fair was on in full swing. Manolete was fighting, and I went to see him in the morning.

To tell the truth, I was shocked by his physical state. He had been out on the town all night "de juerga," and I wondered how he could possibly fight that afternoon. The Spanish public had been brutal to him for over a year now, even though he had just returned from the most sensational season in Mexico and Latin America that any matador had ever enjoyed. He was fighting as well as he ever had, but after a while audiences become infuriated by perfection. They kept demanding more and more of him with every fight. Out of boredom they now wanted to destroy their once beloved idol. Manolete was too sincere an artist not to suffer under this treatment. I was worried, seeing his face even more tragic than ever and knowing of his present bitterness toward life because of personal and professional reasons. He was just thirty but he looked forty-five.

I decided to stay for the fight, and Manolo did me the honor of asking me to watch it from down in the passageway. Once out in the ring, he quickly dispelled any fears I had about what shape he was in by putting up a highly capable demonstration, if not one of his really great ones. But he did many wonderful things that day, things that only another torero could truly appreciate, that the crowd didn't even deign to applaud.

As he came over to the fence to change muletas I exclaimed, "Carai, Manolo, what do they want!"

"I know very well what they want," he said enigmatically, "and one of these afternoons I just might give it to them to keep the bastards happy."

They took a photo of us in the cuadrilla gate, the last together. Then we said good-bye warmly, but with what seemed to me a certain sadness and nostalgia for the great days we had shared that would never come again. As he climbed into his car, still dressed in his suit of lights, he turned and with that hint of a tragic smile that could break your heart he said, "Make them applaud their hands off in France, compadre."

And then he set off, for he had engagements to fulfill. One special engagement was awaiting him, one terrible rendezvous in Linares, from which he wasn't to return, and he hurried off to keep it, almost eagerly, it seems to me now in retrospect.

After my first corrida in Dax I decided to take a spin in my car to relax. I flipped on the radio. With great alarm I heard: "The great torero Manolete has suffered a frightful goring in Linares and it might turn out to be fatal."

The last photo together.

I didn't want to believe it. I had a great lump in my throat as I kept telling myself, This is just what they do, these people — exaggerate torero's wounds to make the news more sensational. But I stayed glued to the radio, and my fears increased when I heard how the great horn wound specialist Jiménez Guinea had been rushed from Madrid because of the gravity of the situation. Then the next morning came the terrible blunt news: Manolete was dead.

I was stunned, empty, parched inside, my spirit shriveled. But he was invulnerable! How had it happened? No bull could kill Manolete!

Rather than my trying clumsily to reconstruct the events at Linares, here is a moving, detailed letter which gives the whole story. It's from Manolete's sword boy of so many years, El Chimo, written to Antonio de la Villa in Mexico five days after the tragedy.

My dear and respected Don Antonio:

I'm answering your kind cable, but I'm in a kind of trance, a trance so great that I'm not really sure of anything that's going on.

You'll have to forgive these badly written lines but in my condition and with my heart in shreds it is hard to see things as clearly as I would like.

My matador, may he rest in peace, went to fight in Linares with enthusiasm. It was the first corrida of the season for him in Andalucía and you know how much toreros want to please the aficionados there, especially those near Córdoba and Sevilla, which are the ones that have the power to bestow or remove fame.

For Manolete the Miura bulls were no worry at all since he'd had some of his best days with them. Balañá, who was the impresario of Linares, had bought two corridas, one

Manolo
requested
the Miuras.

from Samuel Brothers and the other from Miura. Manolo
requested the Miuras.

And they try to say there's nothing to superstition! On
the 21st of August Balañá arranged the fight, number 21

was the hotel room number in Linares, Manolete had fought 21 fights already this season, and 21 was the brand on Islero, the assassin of poor Manolo. These are forewarnings that never leave one.

I left Madrid with the cuadrilla in order to have everything ready in Linares. Manolo, with Guillermo, Camará and his friend Bellón, left Madrid at nightfall in his car (whose license plate began with "21.")

He ate dinner in Manzanares with great relish — you know how he loved to eat — and afterwards he sat around listening to some flamenco records and chatting with a friend of his from Manzanares who kept begging him to fight there. The friend began sucking up to Camará to get him to go for the idea, and to convince him, he took out his checkbook, saying to Manolo, "You put in the amount, any amount, and I'll sign it." But Manolete begged off, saying he had twenty fights in a row and he couldn't accept.

Manolete arrived at the Hotel Cervantes around 12.30 that night. There awaited him Domecq, Antonio Cañero, Bernardo, Carnicerito, and other friends. They stayed up talking and joking until nearly two in the morning. They didn't talk about bulls or anything unpleasant, only about things of the country, horses, and trips.

Manolo was a real sleepyhead. He was a real case. Whether he fought or not the next day, nobody could keep him from getting at least ten hours.

At 10 on Sunday morning I went into the bedroom to unpack the capes and things and to arrange his suit of lights on the chair. "What suit are you fixing for me?" he asked. "The rose one," I answered. "See if you can't find me a pair of those stockings that we used to get in Barcelona," he said, "because those others wrinkle and with the balls of my feet so sore it bothers me."

He went back to sleep, and around 12 I served him lunch.

When he sat up I saw a red blotch on his arm like a bite, and smiling I said, "You must have had some music in here last night."

"A Miura got to me sooner than I expected," answered the matador; Andalucía has lots of bedbugs and mosquitoes.

Then he ate a small steak, some grapes, and a cup of coffee.° He lit a cigarette and went to the bathroom to wash and shave. At one the parade of friends and the curious began; there was his friend the Count of Colombí and the newspaper critic K-Hito, an intimate of his, and the two of them began to joke. At one point, K-Hito, observing the darkness of Manolete's beard, asked, "Haven't you shaved yet?"

"Yes, I've shaved," said Manolete. "If my beard's getting darker it's fear that's making the whiskers come out."

Carnicerito arrived all dressed. "Why so soon?" Manolo chided. "Going to have your portrait painted?" And Manolo kidded him about his amorous weaknesses, which many times had kept him from doing his best with the bulls. Carnicerito had drawn the lots for the bulls that morning and he said that the group of animals weren't too big and seemed manageable enough, judging by the way they let themselves be corralled.

Then came a newspaperman from the magazine *Life* from America with a photographer and an assistant, and Manolo, smiling, said to him, "We toreros are one person before the fight and another afterwards. If you're looking for a handsomer torero, take the photo after the corrida when the resemblance goes back into place. Fear puts a mask on us now."

Manolete was received in the Linares ring with a surprising ovation. Upon parading out the cry of "Manolo!

° Most matadors don't eat before a fight, to make things more convenient for the surgeons, but Manolete became too weak if he went without food.

Manolo!" was heard on all sides. There seemed to be less detractors today. Hat in hand,* like Gitanillo and Luis Miguel Dominguín, the matador stalked across the sand with that style and arrogance which only he had.

The truth is that on the first bull, which was Gitanillo's, there was nothing worth mentioning. Manolo only went out for one *quite* and then the cowardly Miura didn't charge.

Islero came out in fifth place and Manolo, as with his first bull, couldn't get any cooperation from the animal. Gabriel González and Cantimplas barely doubled the animal at all, and then with great difficulty, because Islero planted himself in the middle of the ring and just stood there wagging his horns wickedly, but with no desire to charge honestly. Manolo called out, "Quieto, quieto!" to Gabriel.

Then he opened up his cape and citing with gaiety, he gave it two verónicas with that inimitable style of his. But he soon saw that Islero was inclined to crowd to the right and hooked badly. Manolo tried again, but uselessly, since Islero just wouldn't respond. The animal kept putting on the brakes. Atienza really leaned on Islero in the first picking and again on the second.

The act was changed to the banderillas and in the second pair Gabriel escaped by the skin of his teeth, and after leaping the fence to safety he said as he walked by Manolete, "He really hooks on that right side."

The worst kind Manolo could have drawn!

The matador took the muleta and went out and gave the bull a few cautious passes to feel it out. Then all of a sudden he gave the bull three tremendous right-hand passes, so beautiful and close to the horn that the emotion grabbed you by the throat. The audience held its breath until the pass that finished off and embellished the series, and then

---

* The montera hat is carried instead of worn when a matador is fighting his first corrida of the season in a certain plaza.

they burst out in a thunderous roar. They kept up this steady roaring as Manolete followed this with the rest of the brilliant and suicidally brave faena. And when Islero got its front feet together Manolo profiled himself for the kill just a very short distance from the Miura. He furled the muleta, cocked his left leg, and then, flinging himself on the bull he sank the blade into the withers, centimeter by centimeter it seemed. It lasted too long. You could see him trying to do it absolutely perfectly, marking off the three classic positions of the ideal volapié.

The Mexican public must remember that superb and dangerous leisureliness with which Manolete used to perform the act of killing. Islero had time to wait, to let him come way in and then hook him, snagging him in the right thigh with the right horn. It lifted him up slightly from the ground, and Manolete, spinning on the horn, fell down head

first. An ordinary tossing with no particular spectacularness to it, really. But the horn wound it left! A gaping hole, a hole big enough to kill a horse, from which the blood spouted out like out of a faucet. You could see instantly that it was mortal.

I managed to get out there right away and grab him under his arms, Cantimplas and Carnicerito took his legs carefully and two other helpers the middle of his body. Somebody made a mistake about the way to the infirmary and two times we had to double back. Finally we got to the right door at the same time that Islero crashed over dead along the fence. The bull was black with some white hairs and a fine conformation and a good coat.

The infirmary was very bad, like most infirmaries in provincial plazas. And it became crowded with people. Thanks to Camará and Señor Domecq, with the assistance of two policemen, Dr. Garrido, the doctor of the plaza, was able to start to work on him. Manolo with his eyes very wide open as though they were going to pop out, tried to sit up to take off his pants, but he fell back down on the table weakly. And turning his head to me he said, "This time they've really given it to me!"

Then the help arrived with the dress cape, which was white silk with embroidered red roses, and the Maestro said to me, "Chimo, this time the roses didn't bring luck." And all the time the blood wasn't oozing out, it just kept spurting in a steady stream.

Manolo was very pale, with that yellowness that frightens one. And the doctors began to work on him without chloroform, a fatal symptom for those of us who know.

And the rest that came, why should I tell it? One just watched Manolo die second by second. And one wanted to die also. And the fact is Manolo was able to talk right up to the last moments. What tore one's soul was that "Doctor, my legs can't feel anything . . . my hands have no blood in them . . . I can't see!"

And he was aware of everything. When Dr. Guinea, in whom he had so much faith, arrived from Madrid, Manolete, barely breathing, tried to raise his head, but now he had no strength left and he said with a tomblike voice, "Aren't you even going to look at the wound?"

Dr. Guinea never moved from his side. Seated at his bedside he kept watching and watching him, with an expression of tremendous anxiety. I forgot to tell you that, in view of the bad state of the ring infirmary, Dr. Garrido had ordered Manolete moved to the municipal hospital, which is near the plaza. Only the doctors and Señor Domecq, Camará, and I were there in the room.

The truth is that the doctors did everything possible to save poor Manolo, but the essential thing was lacking: stamina. Manolo was always run down. You might say the tremendous loss of blood simply paved the path for death. When Dr. Guinea arrived at Linares from Madrid it was too late. Manolo went into a dying state early in the morning of the 29th of August and by 4.50 A.M. he was already a corpse.

In short, everything has ended. You must know, Don Antonio, of the plans Manolo had for going to Mexico toward the end of October of this year, set up a house there, and fight only whenever he felt like it, because as far as Spain went, he wanted to retire.

I have the sword that killed Islero. The Maestro had delivered many great thrusts with it, and he had great confidence in it. You might say this last thrust he made just the way he liked to, entering straight and honestly the way he believed a man should. His father had used the same sword, and before him I believe it belonged to Rafael Molina, "Lagartijo." You might say that it was an heirloom of the house.

I am destroyed, Don Antonio, and I'm sorry, as I said, not to be able to express myself better, but emotion prevents me from writing more. With a terrible lament for him who was my chief and my unforgettable friend, I send you a respectful embrace, your friend and servant,

MÁXIMO MONTES, "CHIMO"

I cried a great deal over Manolete's death and I'll keep on crying, because with him not only died a torero in every sense of the word, but also the finest and most noble thing of la fiesta brava: camaraderie. It seems to me that this is an element noticeably lacking in the bull world today.

When I returned from France all Spain was plunged in gloom over Manolete's death. You could see a great sadness in the people of all walks of life and a sort of enveloping guilt, since it seemed that every aficionado felt partly responsible for the tragedy. And well they should have, for my God how hard they were on Manolo that last year! Only by his death could he have made them realize it.

Those of us who knew him intimately couldn't get used to a world without him. We kept fighting the terrible truth, talking about him in the present tense as though he were still around, staying away from the places he used to frequent. But the world goes on and, as people do, little by little we began to adjust to a life without him, knowing that it would never be as good a life ever again.

And then a couple of weeks later another blow. A bull killed my friend Carnicerito de Mexico in Portugal exactly the same way that Islero killed Manolo. Carnicerito had been terribly depressed by the death of Manolete and prophesied that he would die the same way. As he lay on his deathbed he gasped out the very same things that the Spaniard had said before dying. "Doctor, I don't feel anything in' my right leg, Doctor, I don't feel anything in my left leg, Doctor are my eyes open — I can't see!"

Carnicerito placing an extraordinary pair of short banderillas.

Then exactly one month after Manolete's death a bull killed the brilliant young Joselillo in Mexico City — ironically enough while he was attempting a manoletina pass.

I was in a terrible depression because of these deaths, and I even began to think of retiring. I bought a fine estate near Sevilla which raises good bulls from the Santa Coloma strain and threw myself into the remodeling of the buildings and the little bullring, the pool, and the jai alai courts.

But I couldn't relax, I couldn't enjoy it yet. It wasn't just my usual, driving inner self! There was something else very big on my mind. Never had I "convinced" the fans of my country, the fans of Mexico City, that is. I now had earned the true respect of aficionados of every place in the world where bulls are fought except in the one place that meant the most to me. There, I was just another mediocre matador who had "somehow managed to impress Spain with a lot of publicity."

I was determined to show them once and for all before quitting. I made arrangements to fight in Mexico, and then went out on the ranches for the hardest training of my life.

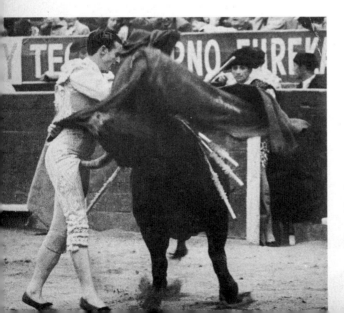

The fatal goring of Joselillo September 28, 1947.

13

My great desire to appear before the public of Mexico City finally was realized when I fought in El Toreo. Things worked out right, and I cut ears and tail off my second bull and managed to repeat that on the following Sunday with another triumph, cutting ears off the first and ears and tail off the second. These were nothing like my great afternoons in Spain, but at least I wasn't ashamed of the performances. For the first time I felt that the aficionados of my homeland began to realize and appreciate somewhat my position in the fiesta brava. I had finally achieved what I had wanted for so long! After so many years of striving and impatient waiting, I had managed to become more than just another bullfighter to them — at least I was now a matador who was discussed heatedly.

I began to think more and more about retiring, since I had nothing more to shoot for in my professional life. Everything I had dreamed of I had managed to get, and with interest. With the money I made in Mexico that season alone I bought a seven-story building on Balderas Street, not so far from where I was born, and another one on Juan de la Barrera

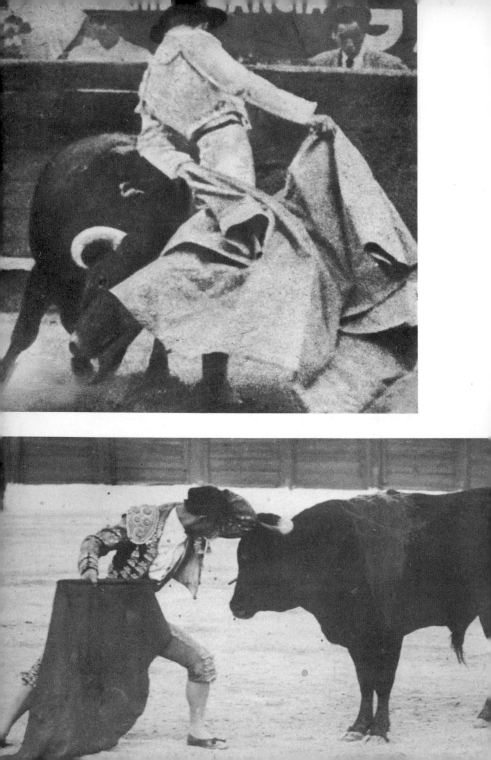

At least
I wasn't ashamed of
the performances.

214

Street. Along with my ranch in Spain, this would give me an insured future; more and more I began thinking about what I had gained through so much suffering and struggle. I was anxious to retire while still young, since I was only twenty-eight years old. One day in 1948 I just up and announced my retirement.

Now there began a period in which the worse side of me began to come out. After so many years of sacrifice and doing without things, I wanted to hug life and the world to me as though it were just about to end. I began to squeeze the juice out of living. Unfortunately my concept of "really living" was neither the noblest nor the most economical. I had no concept of the value of money. I was used to getting great amounts of money for each performance, and now the

Cutting the pigtail off Arruza.

same amounts of money were being flung away, but with the very important difference that they went out in much greater amounts than what was coming in. In between bullfights, for lack of time if nothing else, I used to spend barely anything. As soon as I retired, I dedicated myself fervently to a new way of life. Cars, women, trips, more women, tearing off to Europe for a weekend party, taking along a girl I'd just met, investing in any harebrained scheme that friends suggested — I really overtaxed my imagination trying to think of new ways to throw my money away.

For two years I lived at full speed like this, giving in to the slightest whim and desire that attracted me. The excuse to myself was always that I had been deprived of so many things when I was a bullfighter and now if I didn't really live life to the fullest, what was the use of having gone without so many pleasant things for so long? My cash began to get scarcer and scarcer. Then came the inevitable mortgage on one of my buildings, and later on the other.

In Spain I had a wonderful girl who loved me. I had first seen Mari Vázquez before I retired, under unusual circumstances. After one of my best fights in the Maestranza plaza, I was carried out of the great portals on the shoulders of the mob and swept triumphantly down the street toward my hotel. As we passed one of the homes the grilled iron gate opened and I saw two well-dressed refined girls step out. One of them was especially good-looking, fresh and appealing.

"Hola, guapa," I called out. "Hello beautiful, wait for me!"

She turned away icily. Later I learned she had said to her sister, "Who does that fresh clown think he is?"

"Put me down!" I kept saying to the crowd as I saw her walk away, but they paid no attention to me, and helplessly I watched her trim figure disappear down one of the narrow sidestreets.

Her total lack of interest intrigued me, because a successful matador is inclined to get spoiled by attentive women. I didn't know how to track her down; I tried describing her to my friends to see if they knew who she was, but that did no good. The following day I had to be best man in the wedding party of a bullfighter friend of mine, Antonio Toscano. And then, of course, when the affair began I discovered that the maid of honor was the bride's sister, Mari Vázquez!

At the reception I brought up all my big guns and trained them on this young girl, to little avail. I found her charming beyond words, but she made it quite clear that she didn't particularly like matadors, at least this one. Young and good-looking like Linda, she had understanding and serenity and other qualities I had found so lacking in Linda. She was ambitious also, but I knew it was only the ambitiousness of a normal young girl to be a wife and mother. However, she did not seem to think I was such good husband material, especially after I retired and went a little loco.

It took me some months of seeing her before I could convince her of what a fine upstanding, dependable fellow I really was. Eventually my persistence paid off, because she became as fond of me as I was of her. But I don't know how she stood it. Three times I said to her, "Well, Mari, see you tomorrow," and that mañana was several months later, because I'd blast off for Mexico or New York or Paris or wherever I was going to continue this life that was leading me unswervingly to ruin. Then I'd crawl back to Spain to see her again. She was always ready to forgive me, and I would spend several healthy and normal and happy days in Sevilla courting her before returning to my whirlwind life of dissipation. However, even her patience could stand just so much, and finally she told me she would never see me again, and she meant it.

At last I reached the point where I was virtually bank-rupt; I had gone through quite a bit of money.* There was no other solution: I would have to return to bullfighting. I didn't know how to make money in any other way, since I had done nothing else from childhood; and toreros know little of real work, that terrible word that sends chills through us. I have a torero friend who says, "Carry all the weight you want on your conscience, but not one ounce on your shoulders," and I'm afraid he's right: we're complete losses as far as making a dime honestly. I think what scares us most are the fixed hours of ordinary work, since we're so afraid of that one fixed hour in our lives — the only thing that begins on time in Latin America or Spain, the beginning of a bullfight. To forget that constant threat of our profession, when we retire we don't want to have anything to do with clocks.

So after those two wild years I suddenly broke off from everything that was engulfing me, the women, the sponging friends, the people with wonderful money-making deals that always failed, and I began to try to save the ship. Luckily I was only thirty years old. Nobody knew about my situation. Bullfighters often live a life of bluff; even though they have a fine car and a lot of property, only they themselves know that the property and the car are in hock. I got hold of Andrés Gago.

"Get everything set up again, amigo, it's back to the wars!"

"But we need some money to get started," he said. "And you have all those debts and mortgages."

He was right. I needed a great deal of money. And, oddly enough, most of my bosom party companions of the past two years suddenly seemed to be less in evidence now that the party was over. I didn't quite know to whom to turn

* Characteristically modest; Carlos' splendid talent for spending worked out to be approximately $1500 American dollars a day for two years, which isn't easy unless one really concentrates on the task.

for the very large amount I needed. I was getting desperate, when one day on the street I bumped into Manolo Dos Santos, the fine and simpático Portuguese torero.

"You have a long face, Matador," he said.

I told him of my predicament.

"Here," he said pleasantly, reaching for his wallet.

I managed a laugh. "You don't understand, Manolo. I need almost half a million pesos."

"Half a million!" But he blinked only slightly, borrowed my pen, took a check from his wallet, and wrote it out. "There," he said.

"But I can't take this from you."

"Why not?" he said. "I had a good season last year, and you'll have a good one this year."

My drive, which had been dissipated for two years, was once more channeled, but for two specific goals now: one to make enough money to pay back Dos Santos, the other to put myself in a position where I could beg Mari Vázquez's pardon and ask her to marry me.

My inopportune return to the ring caused a tremendous upset in my family. They thought it was madness to return, since not even my mother had an inkling about my economic situation. It was hard work to convince her of the fact that I had to go back to my trade. She didn't want to believe me. She insisted that I set to work on my ranch in Sevilla and get out of my difficulties this way. A splendid solution, but it was just too late now. My mother offered to lend me all I needed, but I couldn't accept it. That was her money. I'd given it to her. I'd got myself into this mess, and I thought it was up to me to get myself out.

So after two years, before the frightened eyes of my mother, I once again dressed myself in the silk and gold. Months before, I had put on the suit of lights, but that had been for the filming of a moving picture about bullfighting, and of course that was completely different from the responsibility of getting out in front of a real audience. But now, here in Venezuela, I was dying of fear. It was fear of the bull, of the public, of my own aging reflexes, of the responsibility, and the knowing that both in Mexico and Spain many people were waiting to see what I would do in my comeback.

We arrived at the bullring. After a few moments of waiting, the almost forgotten *tara-tara-rí*, *tara-tara-rí* of the trumpet sounded so familiar that for a moment it seemed it had never stopped resounding in my ears. I was fortunate that first afternoon, since I cut an ear on each of my bulls. The other toreros, Dos Santos and Manolo González, also cut ears, and the mere fact that an old man like me could hold his own with these young stars pleased me enormously.

"I'll have that money back to you in no time," I called over to Dos Santos jubilantly.

"Who's worried?" he answered.

That night I lay awake thinking that perhaps little by little I could get back to where I had been in the bullfighting world. I certainly couldn't complain about my first appearance.

The second performance was not anywhere near as good, from the public's standpoint, but I think I came out happier, since we were dealing with a difficult lot of bulls, and one really had to work, not to triumph, but just to keep from looking ridiculous with them. The majority of the time the public doesn't leave the ring very happy with this type of a fight, but the bullfighter does, because he understands the true difficulty of the bulls, and how hard it is to give them their proper type of fight. Even though not hearing one bit of applause, inside the bullfighter is completely happy. I'm sure the same thing must occur to a writer or artist who, although the public rejects a certain book or painting, knows in his heart that it is a better job than one of his best-sellers or prize-winning paintings.

From there we went on to Colombia, and in Bogotá one of those strange things linked with superstition happened. I've always had an aversion to purple uniforms, since two of my bad gorings were when wearing that color. But for my comeback they had sent me three new expensive suits of light from Spain and one of them was purple and gold.

"Throw it away," I said when I saw it.

"Do you realize what that cost?" said Gago, thinking like a manager. "Besides it isn't really purple — it's more sunset violet."

"It looks purple to me."

"No," said the always persuasive Gago. "It's the light. It's not purple, I guarantee you. I would say this was more El Greco rose."

Andrés Gago could talk anybody into anything, and in a short time he had me believing that this material wasn't even close to purple in the color spectrum and that all superstition was silly. As my fat and loyal banderillero, Cerrillo, helped me into the still newly stiff costume I said, "Once and for all I'm going to prove that this superstition business is childish. What could a color have to do with success or failure?"

Just before making the parade into the ring, I said to Cerrillo, "I wish it were seven o'clock and we were all having dinner."

He laughed and said, "Forget it; everything'll be fine."

And everything did start out fine. I did pretty well with the cape and the banderillas, and the applause made me forget the color of my suit. On the last pair I went out in the center of the ring where the bull was, and decided to place the banderillas from a very short distance. Suddenly, without warning, the bull charged before I was ready. I lunged

The bull charged before I was ready.

off to the side, and placed the sticks right where they should go. But as I did, I felt a searing pain, and the red-hot poker of his horn ripped into the flesh of my right thigh. He slammed me back, and I crashed down against the fence. I was stunned. He whirled on me, hooked me again, and tossed me so high and with such force that I was thrown over the five-foot fence and into the alleyway. Staggering to my feet, I looked down and saw that my entire thigh had been perforated by the horn. It was a pretty little gash, and I saw my life pumping out of it in red gushes. They picked me up and rushed me to the infirmary as fast as they could, and then my real troubles began.

"Where the hell's the doctor?" said Cerrillo as they took me in and laid me on the operating table.

In a few moments the doctor arrived and bent over me to see what was wrong.

"Well, well," he mumbled. "Li'l accident?"

I realized that he was dead drunk.

"Bad," he stared blearily at the wound and shook his head. "Gonna 'nesthetize you."

"That won't be necessary," I managed to gasp out. "Just breathe on me a few more times!"

"Gotta put you to sleep," said the doctor.

"Like hell you are," said Cerrillo, pushing him away. Then he called an ambulance. While we were waiting, Cerrillo himself bandaged up the wound and frantically tried to stop the bleeding. He tried making several jokes but his good, fat face looked worried.

Once in the ambulance, I heard Cerrillo say, "Take us to the best hospital — and drive like the devil — this man's bleeding to death!"

We arrived at a large fancy building soon and parked in the emergency entrance. Nobody was there.

"Don't worry, Carlos," said Cerrillo. "I'll find somebody."

Cerrillo, still in his suit of lights, raced through the corridors and finally collared two orderlies. They took me out of the ambulance, and put me on a guerney, but they refused to take me into the operating room until I had made a down payment!

Two men in bullfighting costumes aren't likely to have money in their pockets, even if suits of lights had pockets. Cerrillo exploded, but they wouldn't budge. He ran to a phone and got the impresario of the bullring to talk to the people in the hospital, and with the money guaranteed, they wheeled me into the operating room and put me on the table.

"Send the doctor in immediately!" Cerrillo ordered.

I was flooding the table with blood.

"Ah, that's the thing," said one of the orderlies. "There is no doctor."

"No doctor!" Cerrillo roared.

The men shrugged. "Sunday."

At this point I was very weak, the wound was going cold, and the pain was terrible.

Cerrillo, bathed in sweat, patted my shoulder. "Don't worry Carlos, I'll do something."

He ran out into the hall. After what seemed like an eternity he came back with a young man by the arm. "I got a doctor!" he said triumphantly.

"I'm not a doctor!" the youth protested. "I'm only a medical student."

"You're a doctor," said Cerrillo, "and you're going to operate!"

The student looked at my torn thigh. He shook his head firmly. "I've never operated on anything like this. I wouldn't dare. I wouldn't know how to begin, much less finish."

Then Cerrillo suddenly grew grim, and his jaw set the way I'd seen it do so many times when the going would get tough in the bullring. He took the startled student by the shoulders and shook him hard.

"Listen, sonny!" he hissed, "wash up and get on your rubber gloves — we're operating!"

He grabbed a doctor's face mask and tied it around his own head, and then when the student was ready, he said, "All right— give him a local and then take your scalpel and cut along there!"

The young man shook his head and swallowed. But Cerrillo repeated the order so fiercely and looked so menacing that he had to do as he was told.

Horn-wound surgery is a highly complicated specialty, and of course Cerrillo had seen a great deal of it, but still it is a minor miracle that things turned out the way they did. The unwilling student refused to make a move unless Cerrillo directed it. Cerrillo showed him where to cut, how to look for the trajectories that the splintered end of the horn had made in the flesh, how to open up the tissues, how to sterilize every part of the wound, and in general did everything that a top horn-wound surgeon would have done. I remember every detail of the operation, and I can assure you that the most scared of the three of us was not I nor the venerable director of the proceedings, but rather the student, who trembled, stuttered, and sweated throughout the whole performance.

It wasn't until the next day that I finally saw a real doctor — and a good one. With amazement he checked over the operation that Dr. Cerrillo had performed, called it a perfect job, and congratulated him heartily.*

I think that now you can appreciate part of the great affection I hold for Javier Cerrillo, and also you'll understand why, although I don't like to believe in superstitions, I've never worn another purple uniform.

---

* It might have been perfect on the inside, but I've seen the outside. The scar it left looks remarkably like a hieroglyphic on the door leading to Tutankhamen's tomb.

14

THE GORING in Bogotá, after barely having got started on my comeback, was a blow and blasted my hopes of repaying my huge debt to Dos Santos to smithereens. When he came to see me in the hospital I told him I didn't see how I was ever going to pay him back at this rate. He said again: "Who's worried?" His faith in me did wonders. Before too many months I was not only getting around but was fighting in Europe better than ever.

And finally, by the twelfth fight of my comeback campaign, I had enough money to repay Dos Santos completely. I have never felt more satisfied about anything in my life than being able to write out that check and clear the slate with a person who so unhesitatingly had shown his belief in me.

Though fighting all over, Spain, France, and Portugal, I established my headquarters in Sevilla, and after each corrida I would head for there like a homing pigeon. My banderilleros, Aguilar and Cerrillo, began to get suspicious. I had to confess the truth, that I kept hoping to bump into Mari Vázquez.

"But didn't you break off with her?" they asked.

"She broke off with me," I said, "and with the best reasons a man ever furnished."

One day I went to a bullfight in Sevilla and saw her in a box. She looked so beautiful it made me tremble. I thought I saw her glancing my way, so I screwed up my courage and made a sign that I would telephone her. She made no answering sign, but after the fight I noticed that she was the one who picked up the phone when I called her home.

I had all sorts of coy attacks planned, but when I heard her lovely voice with its soft Andaluz accent I just blurted into the mouthpiece: "Mari, I love you and if you love me will you please for God's sake hurry up and marry me?"

There was a stunned silence on both our parts. I cleared my throat, and then, as though the words hadn't been spoken, we formally arranged to see each other that evening. I don't know what I said to her or how I did it but I convinced her of the sincerity of my love and she agreed to speak to her father.

I got up the next day early, rounded up Cerrillo and Aguilar, and told them to dress up to look their best, without saying why. I walked out into the street very stiffly, elegant, and white as a sheet. When they asked where we were going I managed to say, "To ask for Mari's hand."

Ricardo's jaw dropped open. "Well I'll be goddamned," he said irreverently.

Cerrillo shook his head, and then, in that special tone he always used when helping to plan the attack on a particularly dangerous bull, he said apprehensively, "Well, let's have at the father-in-law, and just hope for good breaks."

I was so nervous that I don't remember how I began or ended my interview with Don Lázaro; it must have been all right, for a few days later, at a large, terrifying wedding,

Mari and I were married. Two days before and two days after we were married, I had important corridas to fight in Portugal, which rather put a damper on things, but Mari knew she was marrying a torero and she took this with her usual wonderful understanding.

The season ended luckily with only one minor accident, a broken clavicle in the last fight, and then we were ready to leave for Mexico.

This next year was a happy one for me because Mari loved Mexico and it loved her. My career had never been better, and with a marvelous Pastejé bull named Holgazán, I put up the best fight I had ever fought in Mexico City. Another time Manolo Dos Santos and I made history by killing twenty bulls between us in one day, fighting in Morelia in the morning, Mexico City in the afternoon, and Acapulco at night! I wouldn't go through that again for a million pesos, but it was quite a triumph for us.

The following Sunday I competed in Mexico City for the Golden Ear trophy, and when I won it against the best competition available, I knew I had reached a great milestone in my life.

But the greatest faena of that or any other season for me was the evening when Mari and I stood together before the altar of the Jesús del Gran Poder and became one person.

15

I FELT on top of the world now, especially since Mari was going to present me with a child. I trained very hard for the 1951 season in Spain — too hard. I was overtrained, and my first fight in Barcelona was a disaster because of it. I insisted on repeating the fight three days later, since the Barcelona audiences had been much too good to me to treat them like that. I harvested some ears the second time around and we were all happier. As far as bullfighting went that was a fine year except for the horrible day in Bilbao when I was so bad that the authorities did the unprecedented maneuver of ordering me up to the president's box and bawling me out soundly in front of everyone.

A wonderful little daughter was born to us that summer. Three days later I was fighting four bulls all alone on the program in Cádiz and performing with a sort of inspiration that must have stemmed from my paternal glow. Everything looked very rosy with the end of the season so near, but as I had long since learned: Man proposes, God disposes, but the bull discomposes. So, on September 16, in my twenty-third corrida of that year, my second bull gave me a splendid

1

2

3

4

5

6

7

8

Arruza shows his superb reflexes, managing to fall like a tumbler.

wound in my left leg. I almost welcomed it, because the goring gave me a chance to stay at home and play with this beautiful little child Mari had created. And when I got better and had to think about getting back into training I began to hate leaving her happy little smile.

It was necessary, however, because there was a monstrous corrida in the offing, the now famous fight in Córdoba, where the ten top toreros from Spain and Mexico fought free in order to raise money for a great monument to be raised to Manolete. Gago and I organized this project, and it was a complete success monetarily and artistically.

A few days later I went off to Peru to fight. Mari and the baby stayed in Spain, planning to meet me in Mexico when I had wound up the short season there. Once again in Lima I was bad. Somehow I had started off on the wrong foot in that city and, try as I might, I couldn't do anything to correct it. It was just bad luck. I shall always be sorry about it, because I would have liked to have pleased those audiences. After my last fight in Lima I flew to Tijuana and gave the kind of performance I had so much wanted to give the Peruvians. But that's the way the fiesta brava is.

The kind of performance I had so much wanted to give the Peruvians.

It was in this fight that I first did El Péndulo — the pendulum pass. Intentionally, that is. Some months before, I was fighting a very erratic bull, citing it to charge a normal right-hand pass, when all of a sudden it lunged at me. To my horror I saw that instead of passing in front of my legs where I was holding the muleta it was swerving *behind* me, probably because of some visual defect. There was no time to get out of the way, so I just arched my body forward and snapped the cloth out behind my legs to give the animal a target as long as it was heading that way anyway. The bull grazed me but didn't injure me, and I quickly dispatched it. It was an unnerving happening, but interesting. I found myself thinking about it constantly in the next weeks.

The pendulum pass is created.

Suppose someone could deliberately make that accident happen. If one could get away with it, it would be one of the most sensational passes ever seen. It would all depend on gauging the exact second to flare out the cloth behind one's legs as the bull bore down; that, plus being able to dominate the nerves enough to keep the feet from mutinying, so that one remained absolutely still. This was essential. The man could not permit himself a flicker of motion; all the movement would have to be in the distracting flash of the cloth. There was no possible way to find out if it would work or not except by trying it out. You couldn't *semi*-test it; it was all or nothing. So when I drew a good bull in Tijuana, I swung the muleta like a pendulum behind my legs a few times when I was some distance from the animal to test its vision and see how closely it was paying attention to the cloth's movements. Then I stood out in the center of the ring and shouted at the animal to focus its gaze on the muleta. I waited with the cloth target out in front of me as it came fast. I'll admit I had some sharp qualms for a few moments when I saw how hard it was charging. But I remained still and waited until it was about four feet away. Then I snapped the muleta so that it flashed out behind my legs. The animal swerved, followed the movement, and to my intense relief, the left horn missed my thigh as the bull hurtled by. That day was one of my greatest triumphs in Mexico, and I was glad, because I have many friends in Beverly Hills and Los Angeles who had motored down for it.

Then a terrible thing happened. Right after the corrida my wife called me from Lisbon to say that our child was very sick. Immediately I arranged to catch a plane for Portugal from Mexico City. But first I had to get to Mexico City, since I was at the extreme other end of the country, five hours away. My great friend the matador Silverio Pérez, instantly pulled out his plane ticket for that evening and said, "Here, compadre, I'll catch a plane tomorrow." I got into a taxi, sped to the airport, and rushed out to the field. As I started to get on the plane the captain recognized me and asked for my ticket. Then he said, "This ticket's in Silverio's name. You can't get on."

"But he gave it to me."

He shook his head. "Regulations."

"My child is sick. I've got to get there!"

"Regulations."

"She may be dying! I've got to catch that plane!"

"Regulations."

The explanations, tearful pleadings, and even threats couldn't make him say anything but "Regulations." He just wasn't going to let me on. I had to stay there on the ground, my fists clenched in frustration, and watch the plane take off.

For that reason I missed my other connections, couldn't get on any plane for two days, and the baby died before I even left Mexico.

Upon arriving in Spain, I went straight to Sevilla, where we buried our little girl. Then a terrible sad emptiness engulfed the two of us. We really didn't know what to do with ourselves or how to try to recover from this blow. We began to travel aimlessly around Spain, trying to shake off the dull pain of loss inside us. As we drove around we passed many ranches. Once when we saw the owner of one riding over his beautiful estate with his wife and young daughter on a pony beside him, the yearning inside us was almost unbearable. This, after all, was what I had been striving for since I was a boy.

When we got to Madrid, Andrés Gago telephoned from Mexico to find out how I felt about fighting now. My first reaction was that I couldn't ever arouse enthusiasm for anything again; but then I thought that perhaps our focusing on bullfighting might be a good thing for both Mari and me. A bullfight is such an awesome thing both for the actual participant and for those behind the scenes that it clamors for one's complete attention and leaves little room for one's other battles with life. Perhaps this centralization of problems and fears explains some of la fiesta brava's allure. It is amazing how the importance of most problems diminishes when compared with the immediate threat of a pair of sharp-horned bulls that are going to try to kill you.

Anyway, it was my panacea now, and, to a lesser degree, Mari's. I flung myself into my career as never before. Luck went with me all the way for the next year and a quarter.

But Mari wanted another child desperately and it wasn't God's will to give her another. The doctor said she might never have one while worrying about whether I was going to get gored or not every week. I began to think of retiring again, but this time it would be for ever. I was thirty-three years old, I had some money, and except in Mexico City, where an embittered ex-matador-turned-newspaper-columnist plus the politics of the bullring had created considerable animosity toward me, my professional status had never been better. It was right to quit now.

I arranged for one last fight in Mexico City, on February 22, 1953, the Corrida Guadalupana, traditionally Mexico's most important bullfight of the whole year. Unlike most fights, there would be six matadors for the six bulls, so that meant I would have only once chance to be good instead of two. I prayed that my one bull would be brave and honest.

Just before the fight I called my mother and my wife to me and told them to get the scissors ready, because when this bull dropped, the 1260th of my life, they could start "cutting off the pigtail," the traditional ritual that symbolizes the end of a matador's career. (Of course this is merely a mock ceremony, since bullfighters have worn artificial pigtails for thirty years.) They were so overjoyed they could not believe it, but I convinced them that even if I were terrible in this last fight nothing would stop me from retiring. They would watch me perform for the first time — but on television, and only on a delayed broadcast, after they knew I had come through it all right.

They were
so overjoyed.

It was the last time
I would ever don a
suit of lights.

As I dressed for the fight I was as nervous as a novillero before his first performance. My friend of many years, the writer and fine torero Bernabé Conrad, brought the distinguished actor Gary Cooper and the beautiful Mexican actress Lorraine Chanel up to my room in the penthouse to watch the ritual of the dressing. I couldn't resist telling them that it was the last time that I would ever don a suit of lights. In subsequent years I would occasionally put on the Andaluz traje corto suit and fight calves free for charity exhibitions, but never again would I wrestle myself into the silk and spangles of a traje de luces and risk my life in competition with other professionals.

No one else knew. No one that is, until it came time for the dedication of my bull. I looked up at the great stands of the plaza, jammed to overflowing, and found the bald head of my old friend, the great aficionado Rico Pani. I had told him once that the day I retired I would dedicate the last bull of my life to him.

As I finished my dedication and tossed my montera up to him, he answered simply and with emotion, "I am sad, and I congratulate you." Sad as an aficionado, glad as a friend. These words meant much to me.

I went out toward the bull with more desire to please than I could ever remember. The Torrecillas ranch had sworn this would turn out to be their bravest bull, and they weren't mistaken. His name was Pilgrim and he was almost as noble and brave as Inspector and Holgazán were, and I tried to give him the battle he deserved. He let me put up the best performance I had ever given in Mexico City, and even my detractors admitted it afterwards. I tried to show the 50,000 people in the crowd, which included my old bullfighting teacher, Samuel Solís, everything that I had learned about the science in almost two decades. I did my very best and most dangerous passes with the cape, placed banderillas with all the skill at my command, and with the muleta I spent most of the faena on my knees. I gave them the teléfono, the arrucina, and the new pass I had invented, el péndulo — the pendulum pass. When I dropped the bull dead with one thrust, and the hoarse crowd insisted I be given the ears and tail, I then reached up and with tears in my eyes pulled off the artificial pigtail. I heard cries of "No, No!" from the crowd, and it pleased me as I stood there in

I spent most of the faena on my knees and I gave them the teléfono...

. . . and the pendulum pass.

the center of the largest plaza de toros in the world in the
capital city of my homeland. Many sentimental thoughts
ran through my mind in those moments. I saw myself as a
child, in front of a calf for the first time. I saw the hundreds
of afternoons pass before my eyes, the flops, the successes.
And knowing that it was the last time I'd feel those emotions,
I savored them as I savored the applause.

epiloguε

Now I FACED a new life. Always I had wanted to be a rancher and always I had coveted the splendid 4000-acre Pastejé ranch, which has produced some of the greatest bulls ever to charge a cape. It seemed to me the perfect place for the perfect life for an ex-matador, for although retired, I was still bull crazy and could never completely remove myself from the taurine world. The tame bulls on the ranch I had in Spain would never satisfy me really — not like the wild strange toros bravos of Pastejé. People said it was too costly and not the best investment I could make with my money. But so it might not yield the 10 per cent of invested capital — I never heard of anyone's starving if he had some land and worked it. And what more would I want from this life but to have enough to eat and be able to fight a brave little animal when I felt like it and have a place for my family? (Once I retired, Mari almost immediately informed me that we were going to have another child.)

So I scraped my money together and handed almost a million dollars in cash over for this beautiful ranch. When I took possession of it, I practically cried. It is incredible how

God has granted all my dreams, little by little. It's still hard for me to believe that Pastejé is mine when I look around me now. Aside from raising my wild bulls and cows, I'm busy taking care of my ninety-three pure-bred milk cows and my many fine pigs. I'm also learning to love the land and the different crops that flourish on Pastejé. What joy it is to see the corn, the wheat, and the oats shooting up.

Spaniards say: "In order to begin to be a whole person a man must fight a bull, write a book, have a son, and plant a tree." This will have to do for a book, Mari has now presented me with two sons, and I am learning about the mysteries of tree planting. As far as fighting bulls, that seems less important to me all the time, although I still find it diverting to get down in my private plaza de toros and take on a brave little animal, trying out capework as I truly feel it, without having a crowd shout at me or feeling that I have to get myself hung up on the horns just to please some people who got gypped by the scalpers.

And to satisfy one's ego, there are the occasional benefit

festivales for charity where one can appear before a crowd with old friends like Chucho Solórzano and Silverio and Cagancho. When I do, and I hear the loving crowd cheer my work and hear the affectionate shouts of "Come out of retirement, Carlos — you're still the best!" I realize I retired at just the right moment; better to leave of your own accord than to be thrown out — or carried out. I didn't want them to do to me what they did to Manolete.

I believe that few people have had their lives governed by such a compelling, burning, blind drive as I had. For nineteen years I thought of very little else except how to become the greatest bullfighter possible.

"All right, be a torero," my father had said so long ago. "But be the best or be nothing."

At this point in my life, I have directed my ambition toward being the best raiser of fighting bulls in Mexico, and I shall devote myself wholeheartedly to this goal. But my restless drive is tempered and modified somewhat. For I should also like to try to be a good husband to Mari, a good father to our children, and a good citizen to my country.

photographic
credits

246

Front endpaper: *Sevilla*. Arenas
Back endpaper: *Pastejé*. Mayo

The design on the front cover of this book
is the Arruza brand